Indigenous Law and the Politics of Kincentricity and Orality

Amanda Kearney • John Bradley
Vincent Dodd
Dinah Norman a-Marrngawi
Mavis Timothy a-Muluwamara
Graham Friday Dimanyurru
Annie a-Karrakayny

Indigenous Law and the Politics of Kincentricity and Orality

palgrave
macmillan

Amanda Kearney
School of Culture and Communication
University of Melbourne
Parkville, VIC, Australia

John Bradley
Monash Indigenous Studies Centre
Monash University
Clayton, VIC, Australia

Vincent Dodd
Monash Indigenous Studies Centre
Monash University
Clayton, VIC, Australia

Dinah Norman a-Marrngawi
li-Wirdiwalangu Elders Group
Borroloola, NT, Australia

Mavis Timothy a-Muluwamara
li-Wirdiwalangu Elders Group
Borroloola, NT, Australia

Graham Friday Dimanyurru
li-Wirdiwalangu Elders Group
Borroloola, NT, Australia

Annie a-Karrakayny
li-Wirdiwalangu Elders Group
Borroloola, NT, Australia

ISBN 978-3-031-19238-8   ISBN 978-3-031-19239-5   (eBook)
https://doi.org/10.1007/978-3-031-19239-5

This Palgrave Macmillan imprint is published by the registered company Springer Nature
Switzerland AG.
The registered company address is: Gewerbestrasse 11, 6330 Cham, Switzerland

You know we got rights, just like any other human, we got rights, whitefellas have to stop looking at us like we are some kind of different human, maybe they reckon we are an animal, I don't know.
They have their land, so why can't we have ours?
They got their ceremony, why can't we have ours?
They got their culture and language why can't we have ours?
You know I think about this a lot.
You know I can't stop fighting for my people, my family, my Country, no, I won't stop. That why I'm here today, talking in this court, telling this judge, maybe he's got ears to listen, I don't know. This government mob, I know them well, they've got no ears. Never mind let them be manji *(ignorant), they can't stop me, I got a right through whitefella law and blackfella law to be here…*yurrngumantha karna-wukanyima kurdardi binjawu *(I will keep on talking, I will not stop)*
—**Annie a-Karrakyny, testimony given at the third Yanyuwa Land Claim, 2000**

FOREWORD

The Gulf is forever calling... The Law is vast and expansive.

During the 1970s and 1980s there was much hope prior to self-government of the Northern Territory, Australia, for Aboriginal land rights to be ushered into Federal Parliament, thus providing a legal framework to protect the rights and interests of Aboriginal people in the Northern Territory and indeed across the nation. There was a sense that land rights could support the recognition of the complex nature of Aboriginal people's relationship to their Country. In part, this was achieved by way of recognising communal ownership and providing a means of making decisions about the use and development of Aboriginal land. It also provided a way of protecting sacred sites. But all of this was constructed or deconstructed to fit complex Aboriginal Law into a western paradigm, and through this process, a lot of detail got lost.

From the early to mid-1900s anthropologists began working with Aboriginal and Torres Strait Islander people around the Country, followed by linguists and in some other places other skilled professionals such as economists. Early accounts by some of these experts told of the complex nature of the various societies that existed but that they existed under the watch of government. Fearful of whitefellas, especially in places like the Gulf that had a deep history of frontier violence and now systemic and structural racism, this was the reality for Aboriginal people.

This reality was my reality as well. I was raised in this era of land rights in and around a small frontier town in the Northern Territory. In the 1990s I began working with Aboriginal communities across northern

Australia, which instilled in me the deep interconnection between people and place. But much deeper than the sense of land ownership is the Law in which Country, People and all systems are interconnected in place-based anchors. And as a child I was first introduced to the concept of Aboriginal Law by my grandmothers and other elders. However, of all my teachings, one memory reoccurs in my mind—I was travelling along the Roper River with a dear friend, Gimul Nundhirribala, as he recited to me a detailed account of how the Roper River was made by ancestral beings. He described where the beings travelled, stopped and lived. The Laws and language about them and the kincentric nature of the Law, People and Country—the importance of orality in their application and being in the present, not something of the past, or being static. Even though Ngukurr (where Aboriginal people lived) was the site of a Christian mission settlement, people remained in the realm of their Law and somehow managed to live with both realities.

Over the course of our continuing friendship spanning over 30 years, it amazes me that resilience is not often used to describe Indigenous Australians. However, as you will garner from this book, Law—(Family and Country), knowledge, ceremony, rules, ancestral ownership, spirituality and associated protocols are still very much alive. The authors have articulated clearly in these pages—that 'Country, People and Law exist together'—the localised social, ancestral, ecological and geographical systems that are entwined in place and the people belonging to that place are fact. Many Indigenous scholars from the bush have articulated this complex reality, but in a form that English-speaking people fail to comprehend.

From the 1990s I collaborated with families and individuals throughout the 'Gulf Country'—from Numbulwar to the Northern Territory/Queensland border, across many different but related families. I was also fortunate enough to work with many senior men and women demanding and worthy of profound respect from other Aboriginal people and whitefellas who knew and understood their place within local societies. Some of these people are the authors of this book. Graham Friday and his wife Gloria, whom I was fortunate to have many interactions with and then to a lesser extent Annie a-Karrakayny, Dinah Norman a-Marrngawi and Mavis Timothy a-Muluwamara—in fact amazing humans in the face of adversity and enormous change and challenge. Yanyuwa are viewed as a powerful people, pragmatic and always searching for ways in which to enrich their young people into Law and Country—I have witnessed that through the various claims, reports and the successful Caring for Country group *li-Anthawirriyarra*—people whose essence and Law come from the sea manifest into a ranger program that conducts globally significant work for all humanity in and around their Country. They are charged with the very serious task of practising Yanyuwa Law in a modern context.

Many other senior men and women of this region who are not co-authors of this book are deeply rooted in their Country and shared the same intellectual capacity and concern as articulated in this story—what is written in these pages does not end at the border of Yanyuwa Country. Unfortunately, I see the fatigue on many faces, fatigue from the long and unrelenting waves of colonisation that continue to manifest in daily lives and occupy far too many minds and souls. I remain in awe of how Aboriginal people remain resilient and resolved to our ancestry in the only Country of the Commonwealth that does not have a treaty with the original peoples of that land.

I have witnessed many people struggle to describe the complex connections, customs and beliefs between Indigenous people and our Law. This is particularly difficult when a large body politic operates within the context of western law and jurisprudence in the Northern Territory: the *Native Title Act 1993* and the *Aboriginal Land Rights (Northern Territory) Act 1976* that continues to wrongly describe the connection between people, place and Law (as described in Chap. 3) in order to suit the western legal construct of a rights-based approach to land and kin. In addition, the pressures of mining, pastoralism, recreational and commercial fishermen and tourism alongside generationally poor health, overcrowded housing and a dysfunctional and in many places irrelevant education system mean that there are serious challenges facing younger generations of Yanyuwa to ensure that the Law remains strong and people are anchored to their respective places.

The evidence in this book shows how hard it is to articulate Indigenous Law, kincentricity and orality, but also the trappings of writing about this, as carefully described—the loss of orality and oral traditions, being place based in description and relevant to the features of that place and the many thousands of people that have traversed that Country since the original ancestors created it. Indigenous people are forced into compromise in order to retain Law and Country and we see an emergence of new generations, using technology and communal decision-making under enormous pressure by third parties seeking access to land and waters returned or recognised as possessing co-existing rights and interests for extractive industries that benefit people far from the place of extraction.

By explaining Old Arthur Narnungawurruwurru's telling of Yanyuwa Law, the authors have explained Yanyuwa Law in a kincentric way through an oral means. This important story is also telling of modern western law that fails to appreciate the complexity of Yanyuwa Law.

Unfortunately, many years of experience have also exposed the brutal truth about the chasm that exists and continues to widen between western society and Indigenous ways of knowing and being. There is no wider gap between our respective societies than the topic and understanding of Law – (Family and Country) knowledge, ceremony, rules, ancestral ownership, spirituality and protocol. How we govern ourselves and find peace with our individual selves and our Country (nature) will be a feature of how or if humanity survives into the future—there is much to learn from the ancient knowledge and ways of Indigenous Australians and the authors have laid it out for us so aptly and clearly.

I have known John Bradley and Amanda Kearney for many, many years and have read with great interest John's work from the time he was a teacher at Borroloola and Batchelor College in the Northern Territory. Many Aboriginal students, especially those from Roper, looked upon John as a trusted member of the family architecture in Borroloola. A scan of the many books, theses and articles that both have published with Yanyuwa families over an extended period of time has returned a proportionate library of information to the benefit of future generations of Yanyuwa people as described with the efforts of Gadrian Hoosan and Nicholas Fitzpatrick Milyari.

The authors have laid out a detailed account of what Law is for Yanyuwa in practice and its underlying philosophy. Not only have they articulated the complexity of Yanyuwa Law, they have outlined the amazing resilience of the community to endure and find new ways to keep Law alive, but also to change and adapt to modern circumstances.

At a time when the nation is seeking reconciliation with First Nations people through truth telling, treaty and settling previous injustices such as the Stolen Generations, it is timely that the future of this country embraces, amplifies and empowers Indigenous Law into the future design and culture of our country. This book presents a pathway for that to occur from the most remote parts of this continent. It is of paramount importance that this book's message becomes part of the lingua franca of a new nation, formally known as Australia. Humanity has much to learn from the Yanyuwa of the southwest Gulf of Carpentaria.

Group CEO, Indigenous Land and Sea Corporation,   Joe Morrison
and descendant of the Dagoman and Mualgal peoples,
Australia & the Torres Strait Islands

THE YANYUWA AUTHORS

Dinah Norman a-Marrngawi   Mavis Timothy a-Muluwamara

**Graham Friday Dimanyurru
(1959–2021)**

**Annie a-Karrakayny
(1930–2007)**

ACKNOWLEDGEMENTS

We acknowledge the ancestors and the old people as the preeminent teachers of Law. We also acknowledge the middle and younger generation Yanyuwa who are meeting and practising their Law in the present.

Nakari wabarrangu ambuliyalu li-nganunga li-wankala kala-ninya nyungku-mangaji ki-awarala ki-anthaa ki-waliwaliyangka kala-ninya manhantharra narnu-yuwa. Karnu-yirdardi aluwa kulu kanalu-ngunda wuka ki-awarawu na-wini ki-awarawu, kujika yarrayarrambawaja yumbu-lyumbulmantha narnu-yuwa narnu-wunungu barra.

From a long time ago, our ancestors were in this Country, the sea and the islands; they were there holding the Law. We grew up with them and they gave to us the stories for this Country, the names for this Country, the songlines and the ceremonies; all the strong Law for this Country.

li-Wankala li-ambirrijingu kalu-manhamanthaninya narnu-yuwa maraka-mantharra kurdandu kulu bajingu nganu barra li-ngulakaringu kanalu-ngunda, marnajinganu janu-manhanji janu-wukanyinji kurdandu barra nuwarnu-yuwawu.

Our ancestors were there in front of us and they were holding the Law safely, with an intensity they were doing this, and then we people that stand behind them were given the Law. We are still here holding this Law with an intensity and we are still talking so hard to hold it.

Marnajinganu wukanyinjarra kurdandu alunga liyi-munangawu li-manjimanji nalu-murunma nalu-anma janu-wunkanyinji alunga baki jarrumantharra janu-wukanyinji kurdardi binjawu kulu alu bara bajalu jalini li-manjimanji li-jakudimulu kurda.

We are still here talking to the white people, they do not understand, their ears are blocked they have little intelligence at all, we are talking to them, we do not stop and yet there is no effect, they remain ignorant, they have nothing to say, we feel sorry for them.

Nganthimbala kalingana-nyngkarrinjama? Ngathimbala kalinymaba nyngkalanyngkarrinjama? li-Manjimanji kathalu liyi-wirdinju ki-awarawu.
When will they listen to us? When will they reflect amongst themselves? They just do not know, they still mistakenly think they own this Country.

Na-ja na-burruburru nya-nganuna wuka nungu-burruburrula nuwarnu-yuwawu barni-ngalngandaya wurrbi barra wuka jinangu yurrungumantha janinyamba-linginmanthanima narnu-yuwa na-nganunga nakari li-wankala kurdardi janu-murdirrinjawu marnajinganu janu-manhanji kurda.
This book contains our stories that concern our Law, do not disregard them, they are words of our truth, words that we are continually contemplating. This is the Law from our ancestors, we have not forgotten about, we are still here holding this Law for our dead ancestors.

li-Yanyuwa li-Wirdiwalangu – The Yanyuwa men and women who have authority to teach.

We also wish to give our thanks and immense gratitude to Joe Morrison for writing the Foreword and for always supporting Yanyuwa Families in safeguarding Law. To Elizabeth Graber our editor at Palgrave Macmillan, thank you for trusting in this project and respecting wholeheartedly the process of co-authorship. We thank Fiona Brady for producing the maps of Yanyuwa Country (Figs. 2.1, 2.3 and 3.2) and acknowledge the generosity of Richard Baker, Alistair Dermer, Therese Ritchie and David Trigger in sharing their photographs of Yanyuwa elders. In recent years, the collaborations and the knowledge sharing and recording efforts which inform this book were made possible by funds generously awarded by the Australian Research Council in the form of a Discovery Grant (DP190101522).

CONTENTS

About the Authors

Annie a-Karrakayny and Graham Friday Dimanyurru were eminent Yanyuwa community leaders, teachers, scholars and practitioners of their Yanyuwa Law. Their contributions to this book and authorship are recognised posthumously.

Dinah Norman a-Marrngawi and Mavis Timothy a-Muluwamara are *li-Wirdiwalangu* -Yanyuwa elders and Law women. They live in the remote community of Borroloola in northern Australia and take care of their Yanyuwa Country, through teaching generations of young people and visitors.

Amanda Kearney is a Professorial Fellow in the School of Culture and Communication, at the University of Melbourne, Australia.

John Bradley is Deputy Director of the Monash Indigenous Centre and Director of the Wunungu Awara—Animating Indigenous Knowledges Program, at Monash University, Australia.

Vincent Dodd is a PhD Researcher in Indigenous Studies, at the Monash Indigenous Centre, Monash University, Australia.

LIST OF FIGURES

CHAPTER 1

Conceptualising Indigenous Law

Abstract Law is the most immersive of concepts in an Indigenous cultural context. It is a nuanced schema for human existence, and goes beyond a system of justice or governance as might be the conventional and western understanding of law, to shape and give meaning to all aspects of life. Indigenous Law provides the logic and rationale for life, as inclusive of ancestral and creator beings, humans and non-humans, the place world and all types of natural phenomena. Law instates the relations between all emplaced elements and beings.

This opening chapter serves to establish the context and scene for a sensitive and respectful discussion of Indigenous Law, acknowledging the varied language that is used around the world to describe and analyse different iterations of Indigenous Laws, ranging from Law, customary law, knowledge, tradition, religion and spiritualism.

Keywords Indigenous Law • Country • Customary law • Kincentric • Realpolitik

Law is the most immersive of concepts in an Indigenous cultural context. It is a nuanced schema for human existence, and goes beyond a system of justice or governance as might be the conventional and western understanding of law, to shape and give meaning to all aspects of life. Indigenous

© The Author(s) 2023
A. Kearney et al., *Indigenous Law and the Politics of Kincentricity and Orality*, https://doi.org/10.1007/978-3-031-19239-5_1

Law is inclusive of ancestral and creator beings, humans and non-humans, the place world and all elements occurring within the realm of Indigenous people's sovereign lands and waters. Law provides the logic and rationale for life and puts into relation all forms of being.

But Law is a difficult thing to explain.

It is much greater than words can convey, and often translation into English (and other foreign textual languages) compromises the integrity of Law or simplifies its presentation for those who do not practise it. The translational efforts which carry Indigenous knowledges beyond their worlds of emplacement often occur against a backdrop of inequitable power relations and histories mired by colonial oppression and violence. This bedevils the project of recognition that many Indigenous knowledge holders and activists sustain in the pursuit of self-determination and political and cultural autonomy. Translation often relies too heavily on comparisons of what may be incommensurable expressions and realities, and depends on language that is itself limiting or inclined towards ideas of soft power and esotericism, through which Law is configured as a moral register to support harmonious and peaceful existence. Such is the legacy of popular categories commonly used to describe Indigenous Laws and knowledges, such as folklore, legends, myths and tales.

More commonly, in outsider engagements with Indigenous Law, knowledge is regarded as a soft asset, an add-on or bonus for research purposes or touristification. Indigenous knowledges are deemed discoverable for a curious audience, yet there is no discovery for something that has always existed, nor is this knowledge free for any and all who might like to learn about it. What is met in an encounter with Indigenous Law, and what we hope to convey in this book, is a political realm of intellectual, spiritual and ancestral power. We champion a cognitive and cultural shift among non-Indigenous audiences to reorient themselves in relation to Indigenous Law, by presenting Laws as substantive bodies of knowledge and realpolitik, which are deserving of attention, but which must be respected on particular terms. This is a vital step and might prove to be a useful encounter for those who seek insight on matters of cultural competency, plurality in political life, natural and cultural resource management, being better in relation, ethical imperatives and restitutional justice.

It is in the face of such big challenges and broader political projects that we, as the authors of this book, are attempting to describe Law. The artistry called for in writing this book is one of balancing the enormity of

Indigenous Law as a prevailing, yet often marginalised, global presence and the principles and praxis of Law at a local and intimate communal level. The guiding authorial hand of Indigenous leaders and practitioners of Law from Yanyuwa Country in the southwest Gulf of Carpentaria, northern Australia, facilitates a closer encounter with Law, but as we do so, we also recognise that the emplacement of Law renders every account and experience unique. We attempt to carefully navigate this global and local richness by first providing a broader introduction to understandings of Law in Indigenous cultural contexts.

In regard to non-Indigenous and western scholarly engagements with Indigenous Laws and cultures, there are critical questions to be asked around how such knowledges, derived of complex systems of orality and generational transmission, are suitably shared and respectfully met by outsiders. This book is foregrounded by an interest in the perceptions that have been generated by academics, scientists and western legal experts working with Indigenous people, as to the nature and value of Indigenous knowledges. Western scholars increasingly seek out encounters with Indigenous knowledges as a decolonial option or functionalist imperative. There would seem to be an increasing willingness to acknowledge the importance of these knowledges and their associated Law. However, this shift should also carry with it concern as to the risk of displacement for the Law itself.

Knowledge is best shared through encounters, through relational ontologies which occur in situ, where knowledge and Law can be met, shared appropriately and understood as belonging to its Indigenous owners. Yet when Indigenous knowledges are transported and subjected to foreign modes of analysis or scrutiny, are they not at risk of harm in being disconnected from their living cultural and geographical contexts? Knowledge is held by Law, and therefore Law matters. We argue that a crucial bond must be maintained between knowledge, Law and context, and thus encourage a deeper acknowledgement of the attachment of Law to particular people, lands and bodies of water. This is why we maintain a commitment to localising our account of Indigenous Law to the realm of Yanyuwa Country, in the southwest Gulf of Carpentaria, northern Australia, which is home to several of the authors of this book. We do this so as to highlight for the reader that Law demands localised political authority and mastery.

This opening chapter serves to set the overall scene for a sensitive and respectful discussion of Indigenous Law, acknowledging the varied language that is applied to this aspect of life in relation to global Indigenous representations, ranging from Law, customary law, knowledge, tradition, religion and spiritualism. In addition to scoping the emplaced nature of Law, in this chapter we caution against the tendency to universalise. We reflexively acknowledge our own complicity in this tendency to presume commonality in Indigenous Laws, however offset this by providing a detailed ethnographic account of the localised and regional occurrence of Indigenous Law as it maps onto the distinct territory of Yanyuwa Country in northern Australia. In Chaps. 2 and 3, we demonstrate that Yanyuwa Country, like many Indigenous territories, is distinguished by a system of Law that predates and survives the colonisation of Australia.

The expressions 'Law' and 'Country' are used consistently throughout this book. They have both been widely embraced by Indigenous Australians over the last two decades, picked up as vernacular in remote, rural and urban contexts to describe the two most powerful, and encompassing, aspects of Indigenous cultures (Rose 1992, 2004). In the first instance, Law (capitalised) stands as a linguistic gateway to describe the structures, principles and actions that give meaning to Indigenous lifeworlds as they map out across linguistically bounded and ancestrally created territories. The practice of capitalising the terms Law and Country in this book reflects a preferred Indigenous Australian convention of capitalisation when referring to Indigenous peoples' sovereign lands and waters. We do this to show respect and to highlight the importance of these words and their meanings to Indigenous peoples. It also signals that both Law and Country are official designations and when used often denote the ancestral lands, waters, culture and ancestral origins of a specific Indigenous language group. This also reflects an understanding that there is no single version of Law, in the same way that Indigenous languages have their territorial range (see https://aiatsis.gov.au/explore/map-indigenous-australia for a fully interactive map of Indigenous language group boundaries across Australian). So, for each Indigenous language group in Australia, one can be assured of as many Indigenous Laws as systems of authority, governance and realpolitik.

The expression Country is, like Law, a capacious term which is used to describe the bounded and known parameters of an Indigenous group's geographical, ecological, ancestral and socially configured world. Country can be used to describe a great number of physical environments, and more often, when used in reference to a specific group's lands and waters, its use reflects a relational imperative which distinguishes an inclination towards artful modes of connection, rather than separation; a defining quality of Indigenous knowledge systems more broadly. Kwaymullina (2005) distinguishes Country through relationality and a depth of care on the behalf of human kin,

> For Aboriginal peoples, Country is much more than a place. Rock, tree, river, hill, animal, human – all were formed of the same substance by the Ancestors who continue to live in land, water, sky. Country is filled with relations speaking language and following Law, no matter whether the shape of that relation is human, rock, crow, wattle. Country is loved, needed, and cared for, and country loves, needs, and cares for her peoples in turn. Country is family, culture, identity. Country is self.

Law is embedded in Country; it is knowledge, ceremony, the rules for land and sea ownership and ancestral origins. Law is practical and practicable, setting the rhythm of life. It comes from a time of the ancestors and in many Indigenous Australian contexts marks the very beginning, as human and non-human life was made vital and emergent in place. Law can most intimately determine a person's and community's field of relations, and immerses an individual into a world of connection, well beyond the human. Many have sought to explain this thing called Law, adopting a range of terms in an effort to do so.

THE LANGUAGE OF LAW

We take up the particular expression 'Law' as a holistic term for a range of elements of Indigenous cultural, social and political life. Law as we engage it also relates to broader aspects of Indigenous cultural life including what might elsewhere be referred to as spirituality and protocol. There are similarities and differences that emerge with the various terminological conventions which we include under the banner of Indigenous Law, such as customary law, religion and spiritualism. It is not our intention to critique these other linguistic preferences, rather to gather them under the holistic banner of Law. Law is a term which carries gravitas and we argue is a language that works to shift perceptions of Indigenous knowledges and political life away from a vision of 'soft power' towards one of authority and overarching governance, which lends itself to realpolitik.

Tobin (2014) offers commentary on the state of play with regard to terminology as it adheres to what we are here calling Indigenous Law. Approached in his own work as 'customary law', or 'living law', he acknowledges the difficulty in defining customary law, and regards it as distinguished by ephemerality, which makes it both open to change and resistant to the constraints of written legal systems (Tobin 2014: xvii). It is described as having a basis in philosophical principles and is expressed in a range of social contexts, from decision-making, legal determinations as they relate to land, sea and resource ownership and myriad forms of 'rights', human behaviour and terms of relating, reparations and punishment for contraventions (Tobin 2014). His focus is specifically on the legal status and scope or rather range of applications of customary law for determining and safeguarding land rights, rules of succession, cultural expressions, natural and biocultural resources and knowledge sharing. Customary law is treated as a form of locally-derived governance that deeply informs human rights. This engagement with customary law has many parallels with the approach we take in this book, although as it will become clear in subsequent chapters we challenge the claim to 'ephemerality' as a distinguishing feature of Law and instead seek to impress upon the reader the durability and actuality of Law, qualities that are attributable to its simultaneous permanence in Country along with its relational character that determines the praxis of Law at any given moment in time. As instances in Yanyuwa Country will show, Law does respond to present need and changing circumstances.

Disquiet with the term 'customary law' is acknowledged by Tobin (2014: 7–8), who turns to the work of Borrows (2010) to explain that "customary law is not the root of all indigenous law, which may also be 'positivistic, deliberative, or based on the theories of divine or natural law'". Tobin (2014: 7) notes that this terminology is widely rejected by Indigenous peoples, including one example given, from Quechua activist Alejandro Argumedo, who argues that the term 'customary law' is "inappropriate to describe contemporary indigenous legal regimes, which often incorporate elements drawn from non-indigenous sources". Argumedo favours the term 'indigenous law', a term Borrows (2010, 2019) also adopts (Tobin 2014: 7),[1] for it is considered a more encompassing term, aligning with the full range of knowledge and practice that constitutes Indigenous peoples' codification of the world and the expression of such through habitual forms of governance, orientation, observation and behaviour. Our justification is similar; we lean towards Indigenous Law because customary law does not exclusively denote an Indigenous origin. In fact, Tobin (2014: 2) explains that "Many national minorities, local communities and ethnic groups that resist adopting the cloak of indigenousness also jealously maintain their own customary legal regimes", thus suggesting that the specificity of Indigeneity is not a root determinant of what might or might not be called customary law. In this book we are specifically looking to engage with Indigenous Law and Yanyuwa Law.

Levy (2000) writes of the incorporation of Indigenous Law into vernacular and systems of common law, customary law and self-government. These are what he describes as 'modes of incorporation'. Modes of incorporation have incumbent vocabularies, which in turn have different internal logics, different moral and political implications and different resulting legal rights for Indigenous people. He argues that when incorporated into 'common law', Indigenous Law is never fully recognised (Levy 2000: 297). Dodson (1995: 1) astutely observes of the Australian legal system, that "[t]here appears an addiction...[to] isolating components of Aboriginal law in order to place them in the artificial compartments which western legal systems are familiar with. This process of artificially selecting what is legitimate provides compromised justice for Indigenous peoples". When incorporated into 'customary law', Indigenous Law is left somewhere between parallel to or not entirely subordinate to common law. The greatest status comes when self-government forms the foundation for the recognition and understanding of Indigenous Law (Levy 2000: 298). This may be why, in Australia, Indigenous groups have not widely adopted the term customary law, rather adopt terminology which reflects the specific Indigenous language and cultural groups for whom Law is held (Dodson 1995). Examples of this in the Australian context include *narnu-Yuwa* which is the Yanyuwa language term given to Law, *Kuruwarri* to denote Warlpiri Law, *Tjukurpa* for Anangu Law, *Manguny* for Nyamal Law and *Rom* for Yolngu Law (e.g., Holmes & Jampijinpa, 2008; Kwaymullina 2005; Morphy 1991; Morphy and Morphy 2009; Pawu-Kurlpurlurnu et al. 2008; Tregenza 2010; Williams 1986).

Given this pronominal orientation of Law and its encompassing importance relative to specific groups, the preference is therefore to capitalise the term. Indigenous leaders also make distinctions in how they speak of Law and the English terms that are used to explain this body of knowledge and practice to an unknowing audience, which might include religion, philosophy, big politics, decision-making, stories, Dreaming, rules and ethics. Common themes which come through in Indigenous authored explanations of Law in Australia include that Law comes from a time when ancestral beings created the world; Law is capable of mapping all lands and waters, people, animals, elements and spirits; and that Law is heavily instructional and can be expressed in myriad form—from relationships, in painting, in song, ceremony and in story. Law provides answers for everything, is of the past/present and future, yet is not written down and is not free (Bradley 2010, Bradley with Yanyuwa Families 2022; Harrison and and McConchie 2009; Morphy and and Morphy 2009; Myers 1986; Williams 1986).

Christine Black (2011), an Indigenous Australian legal scholar, has dedicated effort to examining Indigenous Law, or what she refers to as legal regimes in New Zealand, the United States of America and Australia. Engaging with Indigenous jurisprudence, her writing delivers a focus on rights and responsibilities to the land, and provides a distinct approach and definition of jurisprudence in Indigenous terms, that emphasises cosmology, ancient Greek law of physics and *Djang* (a Gagudji language term from western Arnhem Land, northern Australia, meaning 'primordial energy'). Borrows (2019) takes another pathway, adopting the language of 'Indigenous ethics', to shape an examination of the revitalisation of Indigenous peoples' relationship to their own laws. This is organised around the seven Anishinaabe grandmother and grandfather teachings of love, truth, bravery, humility, wisdom, honesty and respect. Borrows's (2019) close attention to a single law, that of Anishinaabe—Chippewa and Ojibwe Law—is what provides for a rich and deeply thoughtful presentation of Law organised by an Anishinaabe knowledge and value code, inclusive of dispositions and devotions that shape bodily and emotional encounters and social and political life. This beautifully pragmatic, empirical approach is what inspires our own approach in subsequent chapters. Chippewa and Ojibewe ethics in relation to land title, treaties, education and cultural wounding, through experiences such as residential schools, are explained through the frame of Anishinaabe Law. 'Law' becomes the linguistic header for an exploration of philosophy, language, values, politics, action, self-determination, survival and power. In this book we aspire to do the same.

Others have adopted a language of religiosity and spiritualism to explain Indigenous Law, rejecting the view that religion remains an 'imperial apparatus' (e.g., Kraft and Johnson 2017: 13; Kraft 2022). While religion is an uncommon expression in discussions of Law in Indigenous Australian contexts, it has found a place in the self-determined language of Indigenous groups internationally, becoming inclusive of ancestral-based beliefs and devotions, alongside contemporary and emergent forms of belief and dedication, such as activist commitments, new ageism, neo-shamanic practices and Indigenised forms of other religions (such as Christianity).[2] Religion is thus treated as a malleable interface with the world, capable of accommodating changes relative to contemporary need and inspiration. Adopting this distinctive language Kraft (2022) examines Sápmi life in Norway, tracing Sámpi experiences back to the 1970s through the lens of Sápmi religion. Her work, rich in ethnographic accounts, explores the reclaiming of ancestral pasts through a specifically Sápmi religion as a form of instructional, emergent and self-determining Law. This draws connections between religion and identity, engaging the expression 'religion' to discuss the organising principles and enactments of knowledge embodied through shamanism, activism and acts of sovereignty, which are considered vivid illustrations of Law and realpolitik.

Performing a similar role to the broad category of Indigenous knowledge, Indigenous religion has emerged a globalising discourse which distinguishes a shared field of cultural interest among Indigenous peoples more broadly, hence its utility in global activist movements organised around care for Mother Earth and peaceful revolutions of Indigenous sovereignty to protect lands and waters. Yet, proponents do acknowledge the many questions which surround the utility of religion as a framework for understanding Indigenous lifeworlds. These concerns include questioning how language of 'Indigenous religion' has allowed notions of nature, spirituality and animism to travel beyond their local cultural contexts and in the process become vehicles for universalised and romanticised perceptions of Indigenous cultural practices and lived experiences. Some question the extent to which Indigenous peoples themselves adopt religious vocabularies to distinguish their cultures and practices. This is where the local heavily influences the uptake and applicability of certain language.[3] As a framework for identifying shared devotions and dedications, religion has also provided the vernacular to speak of autonomy and Indigenous self-determination, as facilitated through a defence and safeguarding of religious freedoms for Indigenous peoples (McNally 2020; Shrubsole 2019; Sumarto 2017).

Religion is treated as a "distinct sphere of human expression that simultaneously stipulates and depends upon hyper-specificity (*this* rock, *this* pipe) while insisting upon universal – or at least otherworldly authority and relevance" (Kraft and Johnson 2017: 2). It is therefore regarded as a language capable of explaining the local and emplaced nature of what we in this book refer to as Law whilst also locating this amidst a broad field of potentials for being in the world. Cognate terms for Indigenous religion include the sacred, tradition, care for the earth and Mother Nature, spirituality and animism. Indigenous religion denotes a particular system of faith and worship, morality and ethics and can be contextualised by particular histories of struggle and cultural vitalisation. Yet it is the particularity of emplacement which once again renders uncertain the applicability of a discourse of religiosity as appealing to all or the majority of Indigenous groups. Take, for example, those national contexts largely distinguished by dominant cultures with intellectual histories anchored in the Enlightenment and a tendency to prize scientific rationalism. Here, any discourse of cultural distinction or human rights that pivots on religiosity and spiritualism will struggle and be peripheralised by the political majority which upholds and lauds objectivity and the separation of church (as a stand in for religion) and state or which privileges certain expressions of religiosity. This has been the case in Australia, a nation which Cruickshank (2021) examines in an historical account of religious freedom. She illuminates the field into which a discourse of Indigenous religion might enter, in the Australian context,

> ...the social norms and laws of the colonies and later nation privileged Christian expressions of religiosity in ways that restricted religious freedom for others. This was particularly true in relation to Aboriginal and Torres Strait Islander peoples' spirituality...Almost universally, colonists denied the existence of any Indigenous religion, claiming to find no evidence of belief in a supreme being among Aboriginal people. Colonial laws regarding private property criminalised Aboriginal and Torres Strait Islander religious practices by prohibiting access to country, which is the source of Indigenous law and traditional spirituality. The requirement that court witnesses swear an oath to a 'Supreme Being' created barriers to the colonial legal system not only for Aboriginal people but for Chinese people, as well as atheists and agnostics who were denied alternative forms of the oath. The removal of Aboriginal children from their families and culture and their internment on Christian missions involved the loss of spiritual knowledge and practice. The purpose of such laws may not have been to prevent religious freedom, but in practice, what was 'lawful' and what was 'unlawful' in the colonies and later nation privileged Christians and disadvantaged or criminalised other religious practices, particularly those of Aboriginal and Torres Strait Islander people.

The language that adheres to Indigenous cultural life amidst the conditions of coloniality is a powerful reflection and determinant of experiences distinguished by hardship or recognition. Our point being that whichever language is adopted to refer to Indigenous Law is telling both of the histories in which this Law has existed, and also of the political and cultural imperative to safeguard Law in the present. Similarly, the language which is adopted by those outside the practice of Indigenous Laws has implications for Indigenous rights and recognition. Words have the power to shape perceptions and it is against such a backdrop that we have considered our own choice of language.

INDIGENOUS LAW AS ANCESTRAL AND KINCENTRIC

By choosing to settle into the language of Indigenous Law, we honour the Yanyuwa tradition of *narnu-Yuwa-* Lawfulness. *Narnu-Yuwa* and Indigenous Laws more broadly have always been in place, for they are attributed to the structuring power of creation and sustenance of the physical and social/cultural world. These Laws have a time depth traced to the beginning. Kwaymullina (2005: 2–3) explains,

> It was Law that sustained the web of relationships established by the Ancestors, and the web of relationships established by the Ancestors formed the pattern that was life itself. This pattern – being life – is everywhere; it exists in a single grain of sand, and is formed again by millions of grains coming together to make desert; it is in spinifex and crow and rock and human and every other shape of life' and is created anew when these shapes come together to form country and when all country comes together to form a continent. Life, and the knowledge of how to care for it, was created at the same time…Country is the beginning, the middle, and the end.

Indigenous Law concerns bodies of knowledge built upon ancestral and technological thought (Berkes 1993; Ens et al. 2012; Fletcher et al. 2021a, b). These bodies of knowledge are holistic, perspectival and grounded in information that is observed with a method that is predominantly kincentric and built around moral empiricism (Berkes 1993; Berkes et al. 2000; Dei et al. 2000; Dods 2004; Salmón 2000; Wilson 2008). That is, the cosmos has an integrity and empiricism that is ancestrally given, and it is the task of the people that are kin to these ancestors to integrate their recognition and understanding of this reality into their minds and actions. (see Berkes et al. 1992: 22; Kwaymullina 2005).

It is not our intention to lock down a definition of Law, nor to simplify understandings of it. Rather, we aim to provide some parameters for appreciating the vastness and potency of Indigenous Laws, and how Law may manifest in the lifeworld of a given Indigenous group at a given moment in time. Any effort to singularly define Law would therefore be, as Battiste and Youngblood Henderson (2000: 35) write, "loaded with Eurocentric arrogance". There is no blanketing concept or application of Law, rather "[i]t is a diverse knowledge that is spread throughout different peoples in many layers" (Battiste and Youngblood Henderson 2000: 35).

In order for insight into Indigenous Laws as comprehensive bodies of knowledge to flourish, "scholars need to see Indigenous knowledge as a new *sui generis* (self-generating) path, as a new opportunity to develop greater awareness and to discover deeper truths about ecologies and their forces" (Battiste and Youngblood Henderson 2000: 39). Battiste and Youngblood Henderson (2000: 41) do however also dedicate time to reflecting on what unifies Indigenous Laws and knowledges; regarding that "[g]iven the existing ecological diversity, a corresponding diversity of Indigenous languages, knowledge, and heritages exists". It has been earlier stated also by Cajete (1986, 2000) that alongside the distinctiveness of Indigenous knowledges that inform Law are some overarching and shared principles. Interdependence and kinship are highlighted in many Indigenous philosophies and considered to be the determining qualities in how the world is understood, engaged with and valued.

Some of the key principles that emerge out of a wider reading of documented information on Indigenous knowledges and Laws include knowledge of and belief in unseen and ancestral powers; knowledge that all things are dependent on one another; knowledge that personal relationships reinforce the bond between people, place, ancestors and all other elements; and knowledge that order and disorder are relationally constituted and expressed between human and non-human presences through actions and communicative pathways (Battiste and Youngblood Henderson 2000: 42–43). Kincentricity also prevails as a common theme throughout many accounts of Indigenous Law. This pertains to the manner in which people view themselves as part of an extended ecological and relational network that shares ancestry and origins. It is an awareness that life in any environment is viable only when humans view the life surrounding them as kin (Salmón 2000). The distance between the human and the non-human or place is reduced through relational strategies which ensure "intimacy among relatives of infinite diversity" (Bird-David 2017: 223–228). In each localised context, these relational strategies negotiate intimacy and distance between human and non-human kin, and underlie the Law which formalises, enacts and monitors these relations, from one generation to the next.

As Battiste and Youngblood Henderson (2000: 9) remark in the opening pages of their work *Protecting Indigenous Knowledge and Heritage*, "from the beginning, the forces of the ecologies in which we live have taught Indigenous peoples a proper kinship order and have taught us how to have nourishing relationships with our ecosystems ... These ecologies do not surround Indigenous peoples; we are an integral part of them and we inherently belong to them" (Battiste and Youngblood Henderson 2000: 9). Likewise, in describing a 'Native Science' approach, which aligns with the use of Law in this instance, Tewa intellectual, Cajete (2000: 41) refers to an intellectual commitment that requires "mutual reciprocity, [and] which presupposes a responsibility to care for, sustain, and respect the rights of other living things, plants, animals, and the place in which one lives". The universe thus becomes a "living breathing entity", "considered to be 'alive', animate and imbued with 'spirit' or energy" (Cajete 2000: 41, 75). Another distinguishing feature of Indigenous Laws is their multi-scalar nature. Laws operate at the most immediate level of individual identity construction and placement into a realm of kinship and relationality, and can be scaled up to give meaning and governing structure to how the entire physical geography and land/seascapes of an Indigenous group were formed, and how they are sustained in the present. There is a spectacular range of praxis in the realm of Indigenous Laws.

Indigenous knowledges, as the underpinning structure for how Law is articulated and practised, are distinguished by their nature as *diachronic, qualitative, ancestrally bound* and *holistic* (Dods 2004; Gadgil et al. 1993). These ways of knowing thus require the building up of understanding over time that is a long running intimacy which leads to diachronic information, crucial for the comprehension of short and long rhythms of life. A widely accepted definition of Indigenous knowledge is provided by Berkes (2008: 7): who describes it as an emerging "cumulative body of knowledge, practice and belief", which evolves "by adaptive processes and [is] handed down through the generations by cultural transmission about the relationship of living beings (including humans) with one another and with their environment".

A qualitative approach to the cosmos of this kind is attentive to the patterns and relations which form or are inherent between elements of life, or elements which make up Country. These patterns and relations are read through multiple lines of communication, including language, relationships, birth and death, narrative, ceremony, seasonal and hunting patterns and other types of performative and communicative exchange. In the context of Indigenous Australian knowledges pertaining to Country, orality is the distinguishing feature of how knowledge takes shape and is transmitted across generations. Oral traditions can have extraordinary longevity (see Nunn and Reid 2016, who date Aboriginal narratives to within 7250–13,070 cal years BP) and are marked by striking virtuosity (Evans 2013: 293). They operate effectively to transmit all range of cultural information across incredible lengths of time, often emplacing knowledge in specific locales and regions. For example, Indigenous Australian oralities have held and transmitted ancestral behaviours and characters, land and sea formation events, sudden onset events such as volcanic eruptions and sea level rise, unusual or fraught cultural encounters with outsiders and instructional pathways for cultural practices and moral empiricism.

Law as Realpolitik

The vast majority of treatments of Indigenous Law frame the Indigenous experience through an emphasis on criminal justice, international law and human rights. Alternatively, dominant themes in popular discourse tend to restrict Indigenous Law to a philosophical category, as bound to principles and ideas, which give it a soft glow of aspirational harmony. Whilst the first is a crucially important thread of inquiry, it tends to step away from the specificity of Indigenous Law as autochthonous, and existing prior to and in resistance of settler colonialism. In the second case, they potentially limit attention to the practicability of Indigenous Laws and their expression through day-to-day actions and decision-making which has physical expression and political choreography at its basis.

Indigenous Law is formative, generative and responsive, thus its outward expression and display deserves considered attention. It is also a realpolitik and lived practice, enacted and embodied by Indigenous peoples in communal and personal contexts. Such a focus on the livedness of Law or the mobilising of Law for contemporary social and political needs is echoed by Pawu-Kurlpurlurnu et al. (2008) who write of *Ngurra-kurlu*, a 'new design' or methodology for living and building relationships with and among Warlpiri Indigenous peoples in Central Australia. This new design builds upon Warlpiri Law and draws upon the five key elements of Warlpiri culture: including land (Country), Law, language, ceremony and skin (kinship). Adherence to *Ngurra-kurlu* becomes then a template for the whole of Warlpiri culture, an efficient pedagogy (way of teaching), a process for building identity and self-esteem, a way of looking after the health of people and the health of Country as well as a framework to create successful projects that are relevant to Warlpiri people. Rose (2000, 2008) and Povinelli (1995, 2016) also highlight the deeper social implications of Law and how it might be seen as working on a day-to-day basis and in the service of supporting healthy communities, as both positive intergenerational encounters, along with esteem building and generating self-worth and leadership pathways for younger generations. Elsewhere Law has been engaged to develop community-based programs aimed at addressing bullying, esteem building, motivation and employment and intercultural outreach opportunities (e.g., Bradley and Yanyuwa Families 2007).

Graham and Brigg (2020), across a series of opinion pieces, write of Aboriginal Australian efforts to systematically describe and assert forms of socio-political ordering and governance. They have identified a number of "central Aboriginal political concepts", including, for example, autonomy (as a relational-social encounter), proportionality (through the scale of relations to others, and the weight of actions in relation to others), autonomous regard (as the way of balancing human being with other presences and keeping relationships flowing when relations are good and when they are tense and difficult) and a relationist ethos (abiding attentiveness to obligations and responsibilities that arise within relationships). These concepts, along with others they identify such as wisdom, ethics and Country, combine to form an Aboriginal political philosophy (Graham and Brigg 2020) and heavily inform a realpolitik. Regard for such concepts and philosophies (or Law) determines dispositions or manners of human behaviour and conduct within the context of a particularly constituted cosmos. Their emphasis on conduct and relational action reinforces the view that, in Indigenous Laws, "not just any kind of relationship will do" (Sutton 2009: 192). The relational imperatives of Law are such that they are best sustained by and through adequate performance (Sansom 1988: 171). Law is the current which runs through the habit of personhood, meaning that one is "constituted through being continually engaged in resolving the tension between autonomy (or, in Aboriginal English, 'being boss for oneself') and wanting, indeed needing, to be with others" (as constituents of a relational world) (Musharbash 2018: 45). As Chaps. 2 and 3 reveal, Yanyuwa Law directly determines personhood, and sets the parameters for a person's entire relational world. These bonds are then expressed through the performance of relationships.

One of the overarching aims of this book is to dismantle weak assumptions and exoticisations that can surround depictions of Indigenous Laws, and to instate the power and influence of Indigenous Laws, by engaging such aspects as their practical nature, temporal and generational nuance, and contemporary expression. Our approach to Law involves articulating a view of Indigenous Law as kincentric and a relational politics of a high order—the artful combination of realpolitik, intellectualism and ethics, all of which are prone to expansive and responsive forms, meaning that the praxis of Law is a highly negotiated effort.

The best way for us to achieve our aim is to focus specifically on Law in place. This is done through steadied attention on *narnu-Yuwa*, Yanyuwa Law, set against the backdrop of a dynamic and profoundly shifting cultural land and seascape that is Yanyuwa Country in the southwest Gulf of Carpentaria, northern Australia. A focus on the nature, status and standing of Indigenous Law in this one community reinstates the emplaced quality of Law and emphasises the grassroots community efforts which have sought to safeguard Law and repurpose Law for community needs in the present. A return to the local highlights how Yanyuwa Law has been and remains a valuable governing structure for people's everyday lives, individual and communal freedoms and esteem building. But before we continue on to engage with Yanyuwa Law, we wish to introduce the reader to the team of authors, led by Yanyuwa elders.

About the Authors

This book is the product of lifetimes of learning, in particular for the four Yanyuwa elders who have taken a central role in the development and production of this work. It is their experiences with Law that facilitate the detailed accounts as presented in the book's ethnographic chapters and which contextualise our account of the expansive nature of Indigenous Laws. Annie a-Karrakayny, Graham Friday Dimanyurru, Dinah Norman a-Marrngawi and Mavis Timothy a-Muluwamara are eminent Yanyuwa community leaders, teachers and scholars. They have initiated and contributed to vast amounts of recording of their culture and Law, and co-designed research projects over time with co-authors and collaborators John Bradley, Amanda Kearney and Vincent Dodd. They have published several books, journal articles and book chapters dedicated to showcasing their maritime culture and the Law of their Ancestors.

The contributions of Annie and Graham come to the page here, sadly, posthumously. Their passing has been a monumental loss to the Yanyuwa community and to the team of authors, who have worked closely with both of these esteemed community leaders and their families over several decades. Annie and Graham are regarded as having been intellectuals of the highest standing. They navigated and sustained continuity in their Law over lifetimes in which change occurred at a shocking and unprecedented rate. This began with the colonisation of their homelands, and continued through shifts towards the advent of pastoralism and in recent decades the arrival of a mining industry. They both travelled to other parts of northern Australia for work, liaised with Indigenous people from across the Country, committed themselves to decades of land rights efforts and led programs to safeguard their language, Law, sea Country and culture for future generations. Their dedication to teaching Law to their young and mid-generation family members and also to non-Indigenous visitors on their Country was a lifelong project, and their contributions are written into every page of this book. Their hard work and leadership in Law underwrite many community-based efforts that continue to revive and safeguard Law. We mourn their passing and acknowledge their intellect as crucial to the inception, writing and publication of this book.

Annie a-Karrakayny, a Yanyuwa woman of the Wuyaliya clan, was born in 1930.[4] She was of a generation that were the last people born on their Country. She spent her childhood and early adulthood travelling the saltwater Country of Yanyuwa people; she traversed open seas and moved through the island and mainland parts of the southwest Gulf of Carpentaria in the company of old people who taught her songlines, ancestral narratives and the nuance of her Law. As an adult she spent many years working on pastoral properties far from the township of Borroloola, which had become a central colonial outpost and rations depot in 1901. When she would return to Borroloola during the layoff season of the pastoral industry, she would return to Country and participate fully in matters of Law and ceremony. Annie was a philosopher and spent much of her senior adult life trying to work out how western law and her own Law might speak to one another. She assisted lawyers, judges, anthropologists, missionary linguists, school teachers, doctors and nurses who came to her Country, in need of guidance on how to navigate local Law and culture.

Annie travelled to conferences across Australia and New Zealand speaking and listening to matters concerning the place of her Law in Australia and as set amidst a global community of Indigenous people likewise seeking to safeguard their Law in a world increasingly pressed upon by dominant white forces. Annie worked tirelessly with John Bradley and Amanda Kearney in documenting her knowledge and ways of knowing her Law.

She passed away in 2007, but provided crucial insight into the Law that is presented in this book.

Graham Friday Dimanyurru passed away in mid-2021 as this book was already in development. The overarching drive for this book came from Graham himself and hours, if not days, of conversation that took place invariably on the veranda of his home in the Yanyuwa camp in Borroloola or whilst moving across sea Country. Graham was a Wuyaliya clansperson. At age 61 he was one of the most senior Yanyuwa men alive, and he held the mantle as the community's most respected cultural broker in interactions with non-Indigenous politicians and officials. He had a remarkable ability to practise the art of realpolitik, across the fields of Yanyuwa Law and whitefella law. This was solidified by his participation in men's Law in his early years. His childhood and young adulthood were spent with his father and other senior men and women, so his knowledge of Country and Law was very strong. He had been the director of the Rrumburriya Aboriginal Progress Association, and head ranger of the li-Anthawirriyarra Sea Ranger Unit, a position which tasked him with implementing natural and cultural resource management strategies to care for the expanse of his sea Country, in conjunction with a team of young and mid-generation Yanyuwa men and women who he inspired and mentored.

Graham embraced his role as community leader for the 'Elders visiting prison program' and as a member of the li-Wirdiwalangu Yanyuwa Elders Group. Graham was highly literate in western land management and had vast experience in public speaking and representation of community needs and aspirations. He lived his Law fully and was one of the most impressive persons one could ever meet. We have continued to work closely with his wife Gloria Friday (who sadly passed away in 2022) and his daughter Adrianne who very much wishes to see his contributions recognised as an author on this book.

With the passing of Annie and Graham, there is a great need to tell this story and to recognise their intellectual leadership and authorship posthumously. David Isaac Birribirrikama, Annie's son, described the important role his mother played in this community and her standing as a Law woman,

My mum was a Law woman, a business woman, she knew the Law inside out and no one could take that away from her. My grandfather, her father taught her all the way through, even kujika (ceremonial songlines) she knew what was going on, she knew her mother's Country right out and fought for the Law of that Country all the way, right up until she died. I think about this a lot, I went through Law when my mum and her sister Dinah (Norman) were the leaders for Law in this place.

Speaking of her beloved husband Graham, Gloria Friday distinguished his high standing and position within the community and as a leader of practicing and teaching Law,

> No one can run my husband down, he is a Law man and people know that, he is holding the Law for his own Country and for his mother. His father and his mother's brother taught him right through, all the details, he knows how to hold the Law, he's a full business man.

Guiding and intellectually leading the team of authors is Dinah Norman a-Marrngawi, sister for Annie a-Karrakayny. Dinah was born in 1935 in the hull of a dugout canoe, and is the last surviving Yanyuwa person to have experienced a formative and young adult life surrounded by ceremony and exclusive use of the Yanyuwa language. She was educated by a group of elders for whom Law was the sole governing aspect of social life. Her worldview is entirely shaped by Yanyuwa ways of knowing. She is a Wuyaliya clansperson, and the most senior Yanyuwa alive today. She is a fluent speaker of the Yanyuwa language, and the primary holder of songs associated with ritual practices and ceremonies, even some that were once held by men. She has given over 40 years of her life to working on ways to record Yanyuwa Law and culture. She has led the land claim and restitution process for this community, taught generations of young people at the Borroloola school in her local community, advised the li-Anthawirriyarra Sea Rangers and guided John Bradley and Amanda Kearney throughout the entirety of their careers. Her intellectual contributions have resulted in numerous books, films, digital animations, songs and rich ethnographic recordings.

Standing in a cousin relationship (*marruwarra*) to Dinah, author Mavis Timothy a-Muluwamara holds a central role in the development and direction of this project. Mavis is a Rrumburriya clansperson. She was born in 1947. Both her parents were very important Law holders and maintained ceremonial life within this community through until the early 1990s. Mavis is one of the longest serving health workers in the Northern Territory of Australia. She has a strong command of her Yanyuwa language and English and has overseen the translations from Yanyuwa to English that accompany the accounts of Yanyuwa Law presented in this book. Mavis is a superb translator and throughout the process of recording Yanyuwa Law, primarily with John Bradley, has made plain some of the challenges that come with translating Law into English. As such we commit to presenting all testimonies of Law in both the Yanyuwa language and in their translated form. Mavis plays a key role in supporting young men and women in her community, and her healthcare training is a unique skillset from which she identifies and ensures alignments between the importance of Law for health in a physical and emotional sense.

John Bradley has collaborated with Yanyuwa families since 1980 and introduced Amanda Kearney to the community in 1999. They both later introduced Vincent Dodd to Yanyuwa families in 2021. John has spent the last 42 years bouncing around in boats on the rivers and sea Country of his Yanyuwa mentors and teachers. He has acted as senior anthropologist on two historical land claims over Yanyuwa Country, worked on issues associated with language and cultural management with Yanyuwa elders and the li-Anthawiriyarra Sea Ranger Unit. He is also a fluent speaker of the Yanyuwa language, and his research is directed towards issues associated with Indigenous ontologies, epistemologies and axiologies and ways that 'epistemological bridges' might be created with western ways of knowing.

Since 1999 Amanda has sought to learn and share another kind of Yanyuwa story, one that focuses on the experiences of cultural wounding that have pressed upon Yanyuwa people and their culture over time. Not content however to stay with narratives of harm and powerlessness, at Yanyuwa instruction, Amanda has also focused on the community's efforts to heal, thrive and safeguard their culture, Country and Law for younger generations and into the future. Together John and Amanda have undertaken a vast amount of research built around community-identified themes, ranging from land and sea rights, intergenerational knowledge exchange, language and song recording, revivals of Law through contemporary recording efforts and supporting programs of caring for Country. Vincent has recently embarked upon collaborations with Yanyuwa families regarding the community's perception of, and priorities for, a rich archive of Yanyuwa cultural materials. The archive, created predominantly through collaborations between Bradley and Yanyuwa families, tells many stories of how Yanyuwa life and Law has changed over the past 150 years and consists of hundreds of material culture items, photographs, recordings and records relating to Yanyuwa Country and Law. Vincent is working with Yanyuwa men and women on what the future of this collection might be in helping to maintain and revitalise Yanyuwa Law and knowledge into the future.

Our collaborations have continued through to the present moment, and in 2020 and 2021, Amanda and John participated in a Yanyuwa-led project on the effects of the coronavirus on life in the remote township of Borroloola (Yanyuwa Aboriginal Families et al. 2020, 2021). The deceleration in daily life brought about by bio-security restrictions and the inability to travel created opportunities for almost daily phone calls between the groups of authors. Whilst seemingly ordinary these phone calls offered "a singular moment of possibility" (Mattingly 2018: 175), where Yanyuwa reflections on the pandemic and the isolation it induced have led to deep reflections on loss of life in pandemics past, memories of old people, stories of Law and health struggles in this remote part of Australia.

The pandemic also had the effect of returning many people home to the township of Borroloola, including those who were living away for work, and those young people attending boarding school. The galvanising effect of everyone being home increased the volume of persons in multi-generational households and drew attention to the differences between elders, mid- and younger generations and their knowledges. Yanyuwa community leaders have spoken with a degree of urgency as to the specific needs within this community, concerning relationships between old and young, and what they identify as pressure to sustain the cultural expressions referred to as Law. Yanyuwa families in the present are asking, what is the place of Law today? How can Law be taught to young people? And how can the memories of old people be used to keep our community strong?

These questions operate as the beacons which guide this book, alongside and in relation to broader Indigenous Law contexts. There are significant parallels in ethos and objectives across other Indigenous lead programs worldwide, including, for example, the *Revitalizing Indigenous Law and Changing the Lawscape of Canada Program*, involving the Indigenous Law Unit of the University of Victoria, the Indigenous Bar Association, and the Truth and Reconciliation Commission of Canada (see Indigenous Law Research Unit/Law Foundation of Ontario 2013). This program is driving an Indigenous Law project aligned with the agenda to better recognise how Indigenous societies use their own legal traditions to successfully deal with harms and conflicts between and within groups and identify legal principles that communities could access and apply today in order to build healthy and strong futures. So too, the establishment of biocultural protocols safeguarding Indigenous Laws and knowledges, charters of Indigenous rights, Indigenous youth programs aimed at adaption of Law for young leaders all speak to the prevailing importance of Indigenous Laws globally. Indigenous self-determined efforts to safeguard and reinvigorate the place of Law in everyday and sacred contexts are vast in number and reveal the hyper-relational nature of Law as it shapes and influences aspects of life such as health, education, land and sea management to offset ecological crises, criminal justice and ethical relations, esteem building and future security.[5] The appeal and benefit of Law in communal contexts draws attention to its applicability in many contemporary scenes in which Indigenous communities are seeking rights and pathways to well-being, multi-generational and communal strength as well as the effectiveness of culturally based problem solving that is generative, in place and does not cost a lot to mobilise (Pawu-Kurlpurlurnu et al. 2008: 2).

Chapter Organisation

This book addresses two needs in the current literature on Indigenous Law and knowledge. The first is to present Indigenous Laws as governing structures for people's everyday lives. The second is to argue that Indigenous Laws can inform more expansive modelling of politics, the relational, governance and leadership structures, by exploring, through a close encounter with Aboriginal Laws in the context of remote Australia, how Law can enrich political life and provide invaluable knowledge for programs that have a direct impact on Aboriginal people's lives. We approach this from a position of deep respect for how Indigenous Law is negotiated, how it changes and can be responsive to need and circumstance, over time.

In an effort to reveal and more accurately present Indigenous Laws as systems of governance, and as powerful stabilising forces which maintain communal order in relation to lands and waters, we will turn to the scale of the local. In Chap. 2 we establish the specific local context for our discussion. This approach is designed to assist the reader who may, up to this point, know little about Indigenous Law. Indigenous Law is explored through knowledge and practice that structures rights to and control over lands and waters, ecological understandings and processes, relationships between   human   and   non-human   kin,   political   structures   and decision-making. Law is not liminal, and is wholly attached to Indigenous peoples' lands and waters. Too often popular notions of Indigenous Law reduce it to 'folklore', mysticism, fables and legends. Through an ethnographically rich account of Law, land/sea rights and succession in one remote Aboriginal communal context, this book invites the reader into an encounter with Indigenous Law.

In Chap. 3 we present a detailed oral testimony of Yanyuwa Law. Through this, readers can start to appreciate Indigenous Law in practice. Yanyuwa identify as *li-Anthawirriyarra*—people whose essence and Law come from the sea. They artfully navigate a body of Law that connects people through paternal and maternal descent to lands and waters, non-human species, elements and other worldly phenomena. The account which is presented in Chap. 3 is based on ethnography which spans 40+ years of collaborations between the authors of this book. It concerns how mainland and island Yanyuwa are connected to one another and how the entirety of this physical land and seascape is held through paternal and maternal descent. The account details an event in which matters of succession were decided upon, and then maps how these decisions have carried over through time into the present. In doing so it examines the stabilising quality of Yanyuwa Law, and reflects on some of the challenges that have compromised the practice of Law in this Indigenous community.

Our engagement with Yanyuwa Law bridges a timeline from the Dreaming—as the origin point for Law, through to political shifts in the 2000s and the present. At points along the way we engage with key events that have helped to shape and instate Law around governing patterns of land/sea ownership and rules of succession. In the early 1900s a crucial event, the birth of a child, begins a new pattern of land/sea ownership. This child, born to a mainland father and island mother, was spiritually conceived on island Country. He thus became a crucial link between mainland and island Yanyuwa families, and his birth signalled a profound relational bond between clan groups and families henceforth in this community.

Between the 1920s and 1950s this pattern of ownership and right of succession was solidified through ceremony, weighty discussion and collective agreeance among community leaders. In the 1980s this Law was remobilised as the community entered an era of fighting for legislative land rights, and people began to acutely feel the pressure to assert and prove rightful ownership and kincentric order in their community under the powerful gaze of the colonial eye. This has continued into the early

2000s and the present as Yanyuwa dig deep into the western legal machinery that is legislative land rights in Australia. This process has at times been affirming, but also damaging for Yanyuwa Law as western legal processes and evidentiary burdens have scrutinised and misunderstood the Law as it was in the Dreaming and as it has changed since the arrival of white people in Yanyuwa Country. By chronicling this sequence of events as they pertain to Yanyuwa Law, we illustrate the highly political nature of Indigenous Law. This reveals not only the stabilising effects of Law but also how it can be threatened by external and internal pressures, causing community unrest and uncertainty.

Yanyuwa are deeply committed to the specific needs within their community, and at present these needs relate to the passing of knowledge between older and younger generations, a key element of which is the need to maintain successive ownership of Yanyuwa land and sea Country. Many elders have identified a 'crisis in the Law', which speaks to their fear of a loss of knowledge among younger generations of the realpolitik of Yanyuwa Law as transmitted through ceremonial participation and ritual enactment. Yanyuwa leaders have led the call for this book, and describe the challenge they face as follows,

> You know only a few of us left that saw what old people had, only a few of us know how to sing and dance, even the public [ceremony] stuff, we gotta teach these young fellas...and woman too, they gotta know the Law and how it works public side, that's the only side we can deal with now, *kurdu-kurdu* (secret and sacred) side that finished now, that's just for memory, but public side I reckon we can do it if we work together. David Isaac Birribirrikama (son of Annie a-Karrakayny), 2019

Whilst these concerns are specifically articulated by members of the Yanyuwa community, in many respects they are challenges that Indigenous groups face globally, as they negotiate dominant political systems and the enduring forces of coloniality which have swamped self-determined political, economic and cultural processes. Our local engagement with Law is designed to utilise the specific to speak to the big picture. By localising the discussion, the reader becomes acutely aware of the sophistication at play within Indigenous political life and Law in a manner that is more accessible and illuminating. This illustration then allows the book to explore Indigenous Law through examples of kincentricity as a relational modality, and orality as the mode and means to enact and practise political life.

In Chap. 4 we return to a global focus, launching a reflective discussion of Indigenous Law as more than soft power; more than a 'national asset' to be exploited for tourism, creative arts and entertainment. The aim is to make a case for the rigorous nature of Indigenous Laws in supporting healthy communities in the contexts where these Law are emplaced. By extension we argue that there are overarching applications of Indigenous Laws for sustaining healthy communities more broadly. Indigenous Law as a realpolitik will be engaged for the insights it provides on collective decision-making practices, moral and ethical interactions with concepts of land/sea ownership, and kincentricity as a relational expression of high political order.

In closing the book, we offer up a short conclusion and revisit our original aim, that is, to redress a stubborn tendency to constrain Indigenous Laws under the banner of esotericism, which traps them on the margin of contemporary political life and democratic process and undermines their power to influence.

Notes

1. Tobin (2014: 7–9) provides a review of other terminology and its varied use internationally, including 'legal regimes and systems', 'folk law' and 'chtonic law'.
2. Although the High Court of Australia, in the case titled *Church of the New Faith v Commissioner for Pay-Roll Tax (Vic) [1983] HCA 40, 154 CLR 120*, defined the attributes required for a group of people to be regarded as 'religious', none of the 147 religious denominations officially recognised and listed by the Australian government at Schedule 1 of the Marriage (Recognised Denominations) Proclamation 2018, are based upon Indigenous pre-colonial systems of belief (see Davies 2021). Cruickshank (2021) tracks the particularity of absence in legislative provisions for religious freedoms in Australia, noting the lack of protection for Indigenous people to practice Indigenous spirituality.
3. Indigenous people are using spirituality to describe their Law, in ways not always susceptible to a dictionary-type definition. For many Indigenous people there are four main concepts—respect, complexity, creation and connection—that come together in spiritual practices. It is probably best to think of spirituality as action rather than a thing. There is a concept of motion that transports spirituality from inside the person to an external presence, in the form of Country.

4. The Yanyuwa community is organised into four clan groups—Wuyaliya, Wurdaliya, Rrumburriya and Mambaliya—which are described in closer detail in Chap. 2.
5. Future security is configured as a secure, stable and equitable existence for citizens. 'Security' comes from the Latin *se* and *cura*, meaning 'free from care or anxiety' and the United Nations (2016), Annan (2000) promotes future security as freedom from fear and want, freedom to live in dignity and the freedom of future generations to inherit a healthy environment (see also Eriksen et al. 2010).

REFERENCES

Annan, K. 2000. Secretary-general salutes international workshop on human security in Mongolia. Press Release. Available at: https://www.un.org/press/en/2000/20000508.sgsm7382.doc.html

Battiste, M., and Youngblood Henderson, J. 2000. *Protecting Indigenous Knowledge and Heritage: A Global Challenge*. Saskatoon, Canada: Purich Publishing Ltd.

Berkes, F. 1993. Traditional ecological knowledge in perspective. In J. T. Inglis (Ed.) *Traditional Ecological Knowledge: Concepts and Cases*. Ottawa, Canada: UNESCO, pp. 1–9.

Berkes, F. 2008. *Sacred Ecology: Traditional Ecological Knowledge and Management Systems*. Philadelphia and London: Taylor and Francis.

Berkes, F., Colding J., and Folke, C. 2000. Rediscovery of traditional ecological knowledge as adaptive management. *Ecological Adaptations* 10: 1251–1262. https://doi.org/10.1890/1051-0761(2000)010[1251:roteka]2.0.co;2

Berkes, F., George, P., Preston, R., and Turner, J. 1992. *The Cree View of Land and Resources*. Indigenous Ecological Knowledge, Technology Assessment in Subarctic Ontario Report. Hamilton: McMaster University.

Bird-David, N. 2017. *Us, Relatives: Scaling and Plural Life in a Forager World*. Oakland, CA: University of California.

Black, C. 2011. *The Land Is the Source of the Law: A Dialogic Encounter with Indigenous Jurisprudence*. Melbourne, VIC: Routledge.

Borrows, J. 2010. *Canada's Indigenous Constitution*. Toronto, Canada: University of Toronto Press.

Borrows, J. 2019. *Law's Indigenous Ethics*. Toronto, Canada: University of Toronto Press.

Bradley, J. 2010. *Singing Saltwater Country*. Sydney: Allen and Unwin.

Bradley, J., with Yanyuwa Families. 2022. *It's Coming from the Times in Front of Us: Country, Kin and the Dugong Hunter Songlines*. Melbourne: Australian Scholarly Publishing.

Bradley, J., and Yanyuwa Families. 2007. *Barni-Wardimantha Awara* – Yanyuwa Sea Country Plan. Prepared on behalf of Yanyuwa Traditional owners by the

Mabunji Aboriginal Resource Association. Available at: https://maps.north-westatlas.org/files/montara/links_to_plans/NT/7.%20IPA%2047%20 Yanyuwa%20Sea%20Country%20Plan.pdf

Cajete, G. 1986. *Science: A Native American Perspective.* PhD thesis, International College, Los Angeles, USA.

Cajete, G. 2000. *Native Science: Natural Laws of Interdependence.* Santa Fe: Clear Light Publishers.

Church of the New Faith v Commissioner of Pay-Roll Tax (Vic) ("Scientology case") [1983] High Court of Australia [HCA] 40; (1983) 154 CLR 120 (27 October 1983) sourced at http://www.ais-info.org/doc/informes/1983_Church_of_the_New_Faith_vs_Commissioner_of_Pay-Roll_Tax_(Vic)_(Scientology%20case).pdf

Cruickshank, J. 2021. Religious freedom in 'the most godless place under Heaven': Making policy for religion in Australia. *History Australia* 18(1): 42–52. https://doi.org/10.1080/14490854.2021.1878466

Davies, P. 2021. *Four Yindjibarndi Artefacts: Evidence of Religious Practices for a Discrete Human Community in the Pilbara.* MA thesis, Flinders University, South Australia.

Dei, G., Sefa, J., Hall, B., and Rosenberg, D. G. (Eds.). 2000. *Indigenous Knowledges in Global Contexts: Multiple Readings of Our World.* Toronto, Canada: University of Toronto Press.

Dods, R. 2004. Knowing ways/ways of knowing: Reconciling science and tradition. *World Archaeology* 36(4): 547–557.

Dodson, M. 1995. Opinion: From 'Lore' to 'Law': Indigenous rights and Australian legal systems. *Aboriginal Law Bulletin* 3(72): 1–2.

Ens, E., Finlayson, M., Preuss, K., Jackson, S., and Holcombe, S. 2012. Australian approaches for managing 'country' using Indigenous and non-Indigenous knowledge. *Ecological Management and Restoration* 13(1): 100–107. https://doi.org/10.1111/j.1442-8903.2011.00634.x

Eriksen, T. H., Bal, E., and Salemink, O. (Eds.). 2010. *A World of Insecurity: The Anthropology of Human Security.* London: Pluto.

Fletcher, M. S., Hall, T., and Alexandra, A. 2021b. The loss of an indigenous constructed landscape following British invasion of Australia. *Ambio* 50: 138–149. 10.1007%2Fs13280-020-01339-3

Fletcher, M. S., Hamilton, R., Dressler, W., and Palmer, L. 2021a. Indigenous knowledge and the shackles of wilderness. *Proceedings of the National Academy of Sciences of the United States of America* 118(40): e2022218118. https://doi.org/10.1073/pnas.2022218118

Gadgil, M., Berkes, F., and Folke, C. 1993. Indigenous knowledge for biodiversity con- servation. *Ambio* 22(2/3): 151–156. https://doi.org/10.12691/aees-5-2-1

Graham, M., and Brigg, M. 2020. Why we need Aboriginal political philosophy now, more than ever. *ABC Religion & Ethics*. Australian Broadcasting Commission. Available at: https://www.abc.net.au/religion/why-we-need-aboriginal-political-philosophy/12865016

Harrison, M. D., and McConchie, P. 2009. *My People's Dreaming: An Aboriginal Elder Speaks on Life, Land, Spirit and Forgiveness*. Sydney: Finch Publishing.

Holmes, M. C. C., and Jampijinpa, W. S. P. 2008. Law for country: The structure of Warlpiri ecological knowledge and its application to natural resource management and ecosystem stewardship. *Ecology and Society* 18(3): 19–33. https://doi.org/10.5751/ES-05537-180319

Indigenous Law Research Unit/Law Foundation of Ontario. 2013. *Revitalizing Indigenous Law and Changing the Lawscape of Canada*. Available at: https://www.indigenousbar.ca/indigenouslaw/wp-content/uploads/2013/04/AJR_Brochure.pdf

Kraft, S. E. 2022. *Indigenous Religion(s) in Sápmi: Reclaiming Sacred Grounds*. London: Routledge.

Kraft, S. E., and Johnson, G. (Eds.). 2017. *Handbook of Indigenous Religion(s)*. Leiden and Boston: Brill.

Kwaymullina, A. 2005. Seeing the light: Aboriginal Law, learning and sustainable living on Country. *Indigenous Law Bulletin*, May/June 2005. Available at: http://classic.austlii.edu.au/au/journals/IndigLawB/2005/27.html

Levy, J. 2000. Three modes of incorporating Indigenous Law. In W. Kymlicka and W. Norman (Eds.) *Citizenship in Diverse Societies*. Oxford: Oxford University Press, pp. 297–325.

Mattingly, C. 2018. Ordinary possibility, transcendent immanence and responsive ethics. *HUA: Journal of Ethnographic Theory* 8(1–2): 172–184. https://doi.org/10.1086/698269

McNally, M. 2020. *Defend the Sacred: Native American Religious Freedom Beyond the First Amendment*. New Jersey: Princeton University Press.

Morphy, F., and Morphy, H. 2009. The Blue Mud Bay case: Refractions through saltwater country. *Dialogue* 28(1): 15–25.

Morphy, H. 1991. *Ancestral Connections: Art and an Aboriginal system of knowledge*. Chicago: University of Chicago Press.

Musharbash, Y. 2018. Predicaments of proximity: Revising relatedness in a Warlpiri town. In D. Austin-Broos and F. Merlan (Eds.) *People and Change in Indigenous Australia*. Hawaii: University of Hawaii Press, pp. 44–58.

Myers, F. 1986. *Pintupi Country, Pintupi Self: Sentiment, Place, and Politics Among Western Desert Aborigines*. Canberra: Australian Institute of Aboriginal Studies.

Nunn, P., and Reid, N. 2016. Aboriginal memories of inundation of the Australian coast dating from more than 7000 years ago. *Australian Geographer* 47(1): 11–47. https://doi.org/10.1080/00049182.2015.1077539

Pawu-Kurlpurlurnu, W. J., Holmes, M., and Box, L. 2008. *Ngurra-kurlu: A Way of Working with Warlpiri People.* DKCRC Report 41. Alice Spring: Desert Knowledge CRC.

Povinelli, E. 1995. Do rocks listen? The cultural politics of apprehending Australian Aboriginal labor. *American Anthropologist* 97(3): 505–518.

Povinelli, E. 2016. *Geontologies: A Requiem to Late Liberalism.* Durham: Duke University Press.

Rose, D. B. 1992. *Dingo Makes Us Human: Life and Land in an Australian Aboriginal Culture.* Cambridge: Cambridge University Press.

Rose, D. B. 2000. *Dingo Makes Us Human: Life and Land in an Australian Aboriginal Culture.* Cambridge: Cambridge University Press.

Rose, D. B. 2004. *Reports from a Wild Country: Ethics for Decolonisation.* Sydney: University of New South Wales Press.

Rose, D. B. 2008. Dreaming Ecology: Beyond the Between. *Religion and Literature* 40(1): 109–122.

Salmón, E. 2000. Kincentric ecology: Indigenous perceptions of the human-nature relationship. *Ecological Applications* 10(5): 1327–1332. https://doi.org/10.1890/1051-0761(2000)010[1327:KEIPOT]2.0.CO;2

Sansom, B. 1988. A grammar of exchange. In I. Keen (Ed.) *Being Black: Aboriginal Cultures in 'Settled' Australia.* Canberra: Australian Institute of Aboriginal Studies, pp. 159–178.

Shrubsole, N. 2019. *What Has No Place, Remains: The Challenges for Indigenous Religious Freedom in Canada Today.* Toronto, Canada: University of Toronto Press.

Sumarto, S. 2017. Constitution protection of religious freedom and belief for Indigenous peoples in Indonesia. *International Journal of Business, Economics and Law* 12(4): 44–50.

Sutton, P. 2009. *The Politics of Suffering: Indigenous Australia and the End of the Liberal Consensus.* Melbourne: Melbourne University Press.

Tobin, B. 2014. *Indigenous Peoples, Customary Law and Human Rights - Why Living Law Matters.* London: Routledge, Taylor and Francis.

Tregenza, E. (Ed.). 2010. *Tjukurpa Pulkatjara: The Power of the Law,* by the Ananguku Arts and Culture Aboriginal Corporation. Adelaide: Wakefield Press.

United Nations. 2016. *Human Security Handbook.* New York: United Nations. Available at: https://www.un.org/humansecurity/wp-content/uploads/2017/10/h2.pdf

Williams, N. 1986. *The Yolngu and Their Land: A System of Land Tenure and the Fight for Its Recognition.* Canberra: Australian Institute of Aboriginal Studies.

Wilson, S. 2008. *Research Is Ceremony: Indigenous Research Methods.* Halifax, Canada: Fernwood.

Yanyuwa Aboriginal Families – Norman, D., Miller, J., Timothy, M., Friday, G., Norman, L., Friday, G., Friday, A., Timothy, W., Miller, J., Norman, L., Raggett, N., Charlie, C., Charlie, M., Hammer, R., Timothy, M., Mawson, P., Bradley, J., and Kearney, A. 2020. This is our story: Yanyuwa experiences of a pandemic. *Oceania* 90(4): 34–40. https://doi.org/10.1002/ocea.5263

Yanyuwa Aboriginal Families – Norman, D., Miller, J., Timothy, M., Friday, G., Norman, L., Friday, G., Friday, A., Timothy, W., Miller, J., Norman, L., Raggett, N., Charlie, C., Hammer, R., Timothy, M., Mawson, P., Kearney, A., and Bradley, J. 2021. From sorcery to laboratory: Pandemics and Yanyuwa experiences of viral vulnerability. *Oceania* 91(1): 64–85. https://doi.org/10.1002/ocea.5294

CHAPTER 2

Yanyuwa Law

Abstract This chapter provides the contextual background for a case study of Yanyuwa Law and how this Law relates to the ownership of Country. Indigenous Law is explored through knowledge and practice that structures rights to and control over lands and waters, ecological understandings and processes, relationships between human and non-human kin, political structures and decision-making. Law is presented in this chapter not as liminal but as wholly attached to Indigenous peoples' lands and waters. Too often popular notions of Indigenous Law reduce it to 'folklore', mysticism, fables and legends. Through an ethnographically rich account of Law, land/sea rights and succession in one remote Aboriginal communal context, this chapter invites the reader into a close encounter with Indigenous Law.

Keywords Yanyuwa • Australia • Coloniality • Kinship • Orality

In the introduction to this book, we have examined contemporary framings of Indigenous Law and addressed the tendency to reduce or exoticise Indigenous Laws to folklore, mysticism or an esoteric soft-power. We now turn to a local context to more accurately present Indigenous Laws as systems of governance. We seek to reveal the realpolitik of Indigenous Law and knowledge as held by Yanyuwa people, the owners

© The Author(s) 2023

A. Kearney et al., *Indigenous Law and the Politics of Kincentricity and Orality*, https://doi.org/10.1007/978-3-031-19239-5_2

of sea and land territories in northern Australia's southwest Gulf of Carpentaria.

This book is anchored to a particular case study of Yanyuwa Law and relates to the ownership of a specific tract of Country. The details of this Law are told by Yanyuwa people, and in particular two men, three generations apart. The specific testimonies of these men are presented in detail in Chap. 3, revealing Yanyuwa political decision-making in regard to a ceremonial and lawful amalgamation of two distinct parts of Country, as attached to two distinct clan groups of Yanyuwa people. These testimonies of Yanyuwa Law are complex; they do not accommodate for western conceptions of legal decision-making and they rely upon a certain level of understanding of Yanyuwa Country, kinship and culture. In this chapter, we contextualise the account of Law presented in Chap. 3 by providing an overview of Yanyuwa culture and people's ways of living with and knowing their own Country.

The sources of information being drawn upon to illustrate Yanyuwa Law include both Indigenous oral accounts and written accounts, compiled by Yanyuwa themselves, but also outsiders and non-Indigenous observers of Yanyuwa Law and Country. When studying Yanyuwa Law, one must firstly rely on the oral traditions, including ancestral narratives, songs and ceremonies. In addition we draw on ethnographic accounts, predicated upon over 42 years of anthropological collaborations between Yanyuwa families (including co-authors Annie Karrakayny, Graham Friday Dimanyurru, Dinah Norman a-Marrngawi and Mavis Timothy a-Muluwamara) and authors Bradley and Kearney.

YANYUWA COUNTRY AND COLONIAL ENCROACHMENT

Yanyuwa Country is located in the southwest Gulf of Carpentaria in the Northern Territory, approximately 970 kilometres southeast of the capital city of Darwin, in northern Australia (see Fig. 2.1). Yanyuwa are *li-Anthawirriyarra*—people whose substance and identity emanate from the sea and its influences. Yanyuwa Country skirts the mainland coast of the Gulf of Carpentaria, the delta regions of the McArthur River, the mouths of the Wearyan and Robinson Rivers, and extends over 40 kilometres out to sea through and between the islands known as the Sir Edward Pellew group. Mainland Yanyuwa Country similarly reaches approximately 40 km inland, across lagoon and swamp systems, open messmate forests and savannah plains. The coastal Country is carved by creeks, with saline flats

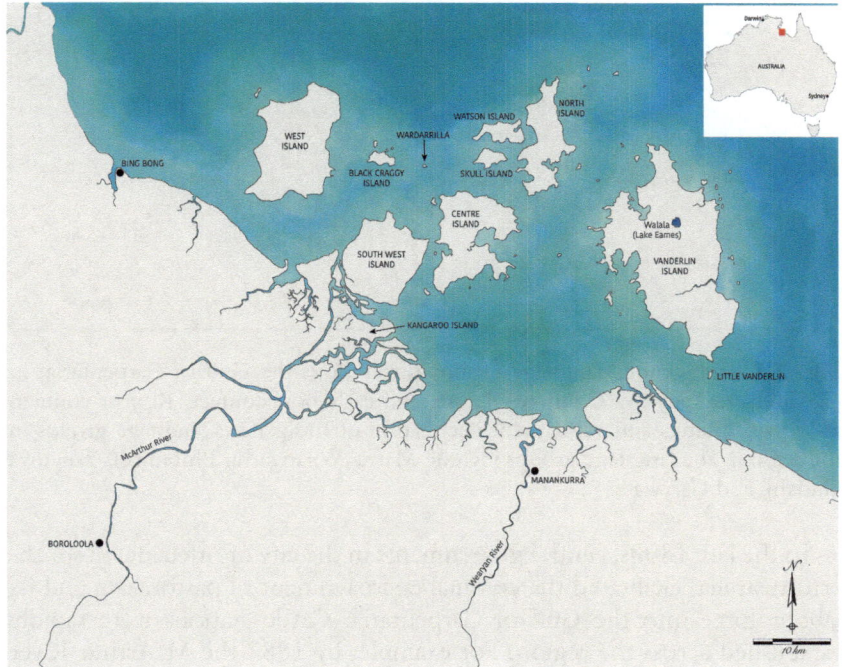

Fig. 2.1 Yanyuwa Country, map of the southwest Gulf of Carpentaria, northern Australia

and dense mangrove systems in between them. Yanyuwa island Country shares these features, along with extensive beaches, sand dunes and rugged sandstone ridges.

Prior to white contact in the mid-late 1800s, there were six language groups living in the southwest region of the Gulf of Carpentaria: Garrwa, Yanyuwa, Wilangarra, Marra, Binbingka and Gudanji peoples (Baker 1999; Roberts 2005; see Fig. 2.2). While these groups often spoke each other's languages, shared Law and had close family ties, each of these peoples also had their own distinct languages, Laws, ceremonies and cultures belonging to their respective lands and waters. The reality of this diversity and distinction between Aboriginal cultures is scarcely acknowledged let alone understood in monolingual Anglophone Australia (Bowern 2022).

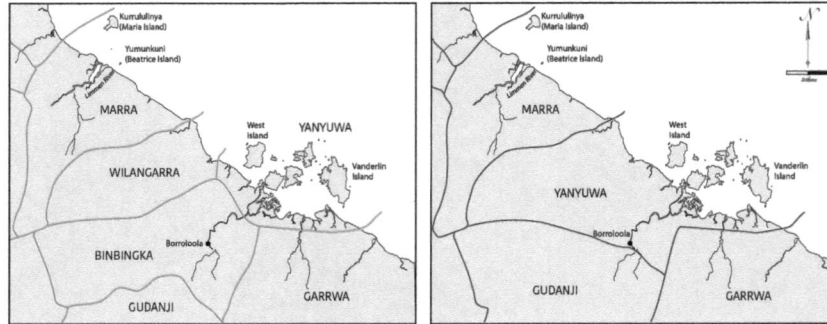

Fig. 2.2 Indigenous language groups throughout the Gulf of Carpentaria, in proximity to Yanyuwa Country—L: pre and early post contact, R: post contact, after mass killings and subsequent decimation of Indigenous language groups in the region. The language groups include Marra, Wilangarra, Binbingka, Yanyuwa Gudanji and Garrwa

In the late 1800s, central governments in the city of Adelaide, in southern Australia, facilitated the colonial encroachment of pastoralism and its labour force into the Gulf of Carpentaria. Cattle stations were rapidly established across the region. For example, by 1887 the McArthur River Station was Australia's largest ever cattle station and effectively covered "the entire ancestral domains of Ngarnji, Gudanji, Binbingka, Garrwa and Wilangarra peoples, and also excisions of land belonging to Yanyuwa and Marra" (Adgemis 2017: 66), including the present-day township of Borroloola where most Yanyuwa live today. Aboriginal peoples defended their Country throughout the late-1800s–mid-1900s. Police reports described a 'warlike state' between Aboriginal and pastoral interests during this period (Avery and McLaughlin 1977: 3; Roberts 2005). Similarly, oral accounts given by Aboriginal decedents of those who fought or died on the colonial frontiers evidence devastating mass murders and reprisals committed by pastoralists and police forces against Aboriginal people who fought for their Country (see Avery 1988; Avery and McLaughlin 1977; Baker 1989, 1990, 1999; Bradley 2010; Roberts 2005). Many Aboriginal peoples across northern Australia refer to this period of colonial invasion and violence led by pastoralists as 'the wild times'.

Being saltwater people, Yanyuwa were able to seek relative refuge from this violence on their island Country of the Sir Edward Pellew group (Baker 1989: 197; Roberts 2005: 174). Others were not so fortunate;

Bingbingka and Wilangarra peoples were subjected to such horrific massacres at the hands of colony-sanctioned pastoralists and police forces that they were effectively wiped out as collective land holding groups (Avery 1988: 206; Baker 1990, 1999; Roberts 2005). By the early 1980s, nobody residing in the township of Borroloola remembered what the languages of these peoples sounded like (Bradley and Yanyuwa Families 2016). Through several generations of marriage and ceremonial alliances long ago, it is now Gudanji, Yanyuwa and Marra people who variously take responsibility for what was Wilangarra and Bingbinka Country (Bradley 1997: 59; Adgemis 2017: 76). The Garrwa and Gudanji also experienced horrific frontier violence, but by withdrawing into their high stone Country, they escaped further atrocities (Roberts 2005; Bradley and Yanyuwa Families 2016: 10).

Up until the 1950s, Yanyuwa people predominately lived across the Pellew Islands and the coastal margins of the southwest Gulf of Carpentaria (Baker 1989, 1999). Assimilationist policies of Australian governments throughout the twentieth century diminished Aboriginal agency and curtailed people's movements around their island Country (Baker 1999). The combination of the dispossession of Aboriginal lands, subsequent dependence upon welfare rations after having been banished and 'brought in' from their own Country, and the integration of Aboriginal families into the pastoral labour force across the neighbouring Barkley and Gulf regions all led to rapid disruption to Yanyuwa ways of life (see Baker 1989; Reay 1962, 1970; Bradley 1997, 2010). Throughout the middle of the twentieth century, Aboriginal families (in particular, middle-aged men) were an inexpensive and sometimes indentured source of labour for the bourgeoning pastoral industry in northern Australia (Trigger 1992). Many Aboriginal people found relative freedom in this work compared to the assimilationist rations and welfare regimes which operated in towns such as Borroloola during this time (Baker 1999; Avery and McLaughlin 1977; Bradley 2010). Aboriginal pastoral workers in this part of northern Australia were commonly 'laid off' during the hot wet season, during which time many returned from remote stations to their ancestral homes to be on Country with family.

While Yanyuwa people maintain strong connections to and regularly travel to their saltwater Country (Kearney 2017, Kearney 2019; Kearney and Bradley 2015; Bradley and Johnson 2015), the township of Borroloola and its surrounding outstations[1] are now the centre of everyday life. Borroloola is located on the McArthur River 60 km upstream from its mouth on what was once Binbingka Country. Today Borroloola is considered Yanyuwa Country (Adgemis 2017: 76; Bradley 1997: 59). Despite all of these social upheavals, Yanyuwa held onto their own Law and, albeit in circumstances of rapid change, it remains central to their own daily way of being.

NARNU-YUWA: Yanyuwa Law, Kinship and Responsibility

Yanyuwa ideals of Law were, and are, codified into oral traditions and demonstrated as praxis through ceremony, song and day-to-day interactions with Country and family. However, like the doctrine of precedent in British common law, Yanyuwa Law has been receptive to change while maintaining conformity with its basic beliefs. Yanyuwa people will refer to what the old people said when considering what to do on matters beyond those which the old people would have experienced. [2] In selecting what to recall, and applying the principles to new situations, Yanyuwa may discard that which has become unpalatable, outmoded or at times even inconvenient, just as is the case, in a broad sense, in the common law. Neither Law nor custom is moribund; the norms and standards that constitute the custom of a society change with it, and Yanyuwa Law is no exception.

There is compelling evidence that custom did not constrain Yanyuwa adaptation and development. Yanyuwa tradition, like western tradition, is always changing, adapting and responding to new needs, challenges and ideas (Bradley 2010). How conflict and tension has been lawfully negotiated in the past bears heavily upon how such conflict and tension ought to be dealt with in the present and future. There is no rule that things handed down cannot be passed on with improvements, or even at times dropped completely. For example, Yanyuwa men and women have in the past made decisions not to pass on certain 'power songs' known as *narnu-nyiri*; songs which are associated with directing or generating harm towards other people or living beings (Bradley 1997: 121). Old people collectively decided not to pass these songs on to younger generations as they believed that such songs had no place in a world that was so rapidly changing.[3] Another example pertains to the use of synthetic western products in the carrying out of ceremony. The killing of birds and use of their down as body decorations for ceremonial purposes (known as *yirriny*) has been replaced by the use of the cotton inner lining of Huggies nappies (see Borroloola Aboriginal Community 1981).

Perhaps the greatest distinction in the Yanyuwa case is the severity and lack of control over the changes in circumstances within which the Law must operate due to the force of colonisation. As we come to discuss later in this book, in the wake of centuries of colonial violence, dispossession and assimilationist destruction of Yanyuwa life and people, any revitalisation of the Law as it once operated becomes increasingly difficult.

At their heart, Yanyuwa conceptions of self, land and sea emanate from their Law. Avery (1988: 3), having worked with Yanyuwa elders during the 1970s, wrote that, "'Law', in short, is the most embracing and legitimating concept for behaviour both at the local level and for the larger social order in which it takes place [...] For [Yanyuwa], law practically covers the whole field of culture". Law is transmitted orally, handed on from generation to generation. Yanyuwa legal authority is substantially gerontocratic, with senior community members holding full responsibility to "keep it going, and to keep it safe" (Mussolini Harvey in Bradley 1988: xi–xii). In Yanyuwa the word that best translates to 'the Law' is the abstract noun form *narnu-Yuwa*. Yanyuwa is a prefixing language, and the prefixes accorded to a root word will convey contextual or interpretive meaning. The root word for Law is *-yuwa*; however in Yanyuwa it never appears on its own in this way. When combined with the abstract prefix *narnu-* which is used to refer to abstract natural phenomena or places of significance, the term *narnu-yuwa* can be translated to 'the Law', 'Lawfulness' or even correctness. *-Yuwa* can also take masculine prefixes—*na-Yuwa* and *ni-Yuwa*[4]—and in these forms are more often used to refer to western law. These Yanyuwa prefixes shed light on a broadly held view from a Yanyuwa perspective that western law lacks a certain vibrancy and creativity and displays a peculiar rigidity. As Annie a-Karrakayny (in 1985) once commented:

> You reckon white fellas are happy with their *ni-yuwa* (law) paper, paper, book, book big words. I don't know, not like *narnu-yuwa*, for us mob Yanyuwa people, got song, dance, Country and got family too, deep meaning you know.

More often than not, Yanyuwa do not refer to western law by a term using the Yanyuwa *-Yuwa* root for Law. Instead, western law is more often referred to by the term *munangangala*—meaning the strangers culture or white people's culture.

Yanyuwa assert that all the elements of their saltwater Country and its Law are derived from the *Yijan*—a time of ancestral activity and creation—and that all human and non-human elements of their Country are kin (Bradley 1997, 2008; Bradley with Yanyuwa Families 2022). In the past, ancestral beings came out of the earth, rose up from the sea or travelled into Yanyuwa Country from other countries belonging to other people. In Aboriginal English used by Yanyuwa families today, these ancestral beings are called Dreamings. Today Yanyuwa Country is patterned with the tracks and movements of the Dreamings: where they danced and sang, left trees and plants, created landforms and left sources of water.

Some Dreamings travelled and then stopped somewhere, setting themselves to rest in that place. Other Dreamings did not travel; some just rose up from the place they were resting and went no further and there they still remain. Dreamings often changed from human to non-human and back again. They argued and fought with one another, they grew old and they left their essence in the Country at specific places. In any case, the Dreamings are still sentient, active and sometimes very dangerous. It is the enduring presence of the Dreaming which sustains Country in the present.

As the Dreamings moved through Country, they called out the names that the Country still carries today; they sang the Country into being and spoke Yanyuwa language into Country. There is scarcely a hill, a river, a stretch of sea, a reef, a bay or peninsula that does not have a name (Bradley with Yanyuwa Families 2022). This patterning of Dreaming paths over Yanyuwa Country and beyond created enduring relationships *between places*, where separate countries are bonded together through the travels of the Dreaming ancestors, and where species of birds, reptiles, mammals, fish, plants and natural phenomena retain an ability to speak to each other.

Whilst the Dreamings are understood to have done this in a period of creation, their actions are not relinquished to the past; their agency is very much of the present moment. The forms that Dreamings take go beyond the geographical features that they created or mark their enduring resting place. Dreamings manifest as animals and meteorological phenomena (such as the North Wind or a waterspout) which are equally known to be their living embodiments which move through Country still.

The Dreamings are not abstract entities for Yanyuwa: they are kin, and their living, meteorological and geographical forms that still inhabit Country are also kin. The kincentric understanding of Dreamings position them as ancestors for Yanyuwa people. Thus, Yanyuwa Country and the Law which governs it are saturated with relational entanglements between people, ancestors, non-human kin and Dreamings. The Dreamings are still spoken to on a daily basis, as one would address kin (Bradley with Yanyuwa Families 2022; Kearney 2021). There are four primary lines of descent when addressing the Dreaming as kin. These referential terms are employed to claim kinship not only to the Dreamings themselves but to Country, flora, fauna, natural phenomena, ceremonies and material culture items. These important four lines of descent are,

ja-murimiri – my most senior paternal kin
ja-yakurra – my mother's Dreaming
ja-wukuku – my most senior mother's mother's brother
ja-ngabuji – my most senior father's mother's brother's Country

There is no equivalent of the phrase 'I own' in Yanyuwa language. People are Country; thus a greater inseparability exists than could ever be accommodated by a logic of 'owning'—as understood in a western possessive sense. The expression *manhantharra awara* can be translated as 'holding Country'. To hold the Dreaming as kin is to hold Country, and in a Yanyuwa sense this term for 'holding Country' is as close as Yanyuwa comes to the English statement 'I own Country'. All of this is sustained through a political system of kin (detailed below). Through the actions of human kin having regard for non-human kin, Country becomes an exercise in the functioning of Yanyuwa Law.

In all cultures there are people who are said to 'break the law', to have 'no concern for the rules' as Yanyuwa might say. The word in Yanyuwa for errant behaviour in matters of Law is *kabarrkabarr* which best translates to being truly stupid, a vandal or destructive of order. There is a phrase that is used for people who disregard the Law and the trouble it makes—*jalu-yabimanji budijbudij awara li-ngajbirrinjarra*—meaning 'they are making a troubled Country, they are doubters'.

Law, people and Country are all part of a relational circle, whereby *narnu-Yuwa*, Lawfulness, is the epistemological underpinning that allows people and knowledge of Country to continuously interact, to act mutually and in consideration of each other. Yanyuwa elder Mussolini Harvey once explained how the ancestral past of Yanyuwa Country is the very basis of Yanyuwa Law (Bradley 1988: xi–xii).

White people ask us all the time, what is Dreaming? This is a hard question because Dreaming is a really big thing for Aboriginal people. In our language, Yanyuwa, we call the Dreaming *Yijan*. The Dreamings made our Law or *narnu-Yuwa*. This Law is the way we live our rules. This Law is our ceremonies, our songs, our stories; all of these things came from the Dreaming. The Dreamings are our ancestors, no matter if they are fish, birds, men, women, animals, wind or rain. All things in our country have Law, they have ceremony and song, and they have people who are related to them.

Mussolini's statement indicates that a profound interconnectivity between people, non-human presences and place lies at the heart of Yanyuwa Law.

KINCENTRIC ORDER: YANYUWA POLITICS OF LAND AND SEA OWNERSHIP

Yanyuwa relationships with their saltwater Country illustrate kincentric order and kincentric ecology. Kincentricity is a view of "humans and nature as part of an extended ecological family that shares ancestry and origins" (Salmón 2000; Senos et al. 2006: 397), whereby "the world is not one of wonder, but rather familiarity" (Salmón 2000: 1332). Kincentricity is a form of interconnectedness to "all that is relatable" (Senos et al. 2006: 397), where human life is in a systemic relationship with a range of other tangible presences such as place, non-human animals, meteorological phenomena and intangible presences such as the aforementioned Dreamings and the spirits of deceased kin that inhabit Country.[5] This form of kinship entails familial responsibility across all species and environments on an everyday basis; human and non-human presences on Country are both consequential and exist in a web of relationships between one another.

A fundamental element of the kincentric organisation of Yanyuwa people and Country is a system of four patrilineal Yanyuwa clans—Rrumburriya, Mambaliya-Wawukarriya, Wuyaliya and Wurdaliya. Each of these Yanyuwa clans carries rights and responsibilities over certain ceremonies, places and species (Bradley 1997: 140–145 Bradley 2010; Bradley with Yanyuwa Families 2022, see Fig. 2.3 and Table 2.1). This kinship system extends beyond human-to-human relationships and responsibilities; all elements of Yanyuwa Country—environmental phenomena, plants and animals— are aligned to these same four clan group (Bradley 2008, 2021; Bradley and Kearney 2018; Yanyuwa Families et al. 2003). This includes clan-based responsibility for specific areas of marine and terrestrial Country.

This patrilineal kinship system assigns individual people to the status of *ngimarringki*, meaning owner or what is referred to as 'boss for Country' in Aboriginal English (Bradley and Yanyuwa Families 2017: 419, Bradley

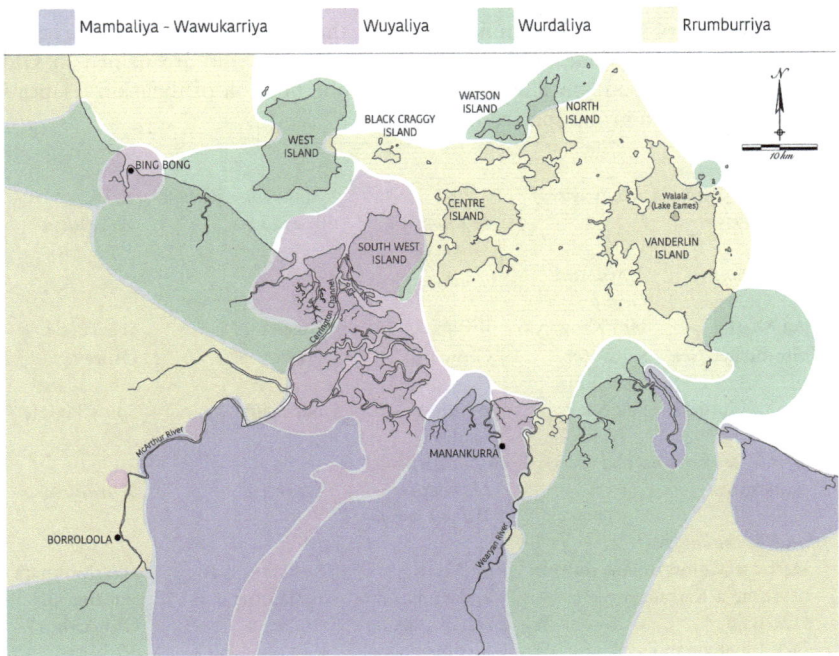

| Mambaliya - Wawukarriya | Wuyaliya | Wurdaliya | Rrumburriya |

Fig. 2.3 Map showing clan distinctions across Yanyuwa Country

with Yanyuwa Families 2022: 80–91). Individuals inherit responsibility as *ngimarringki* for their father's Country. Similarly assigned is the status of *jungkayi*, who are ritual managers or guardians for specific land and ceremonies associated with their mother's Country. *Jungkayi* are often referred to as the 'policemen for Country' in Aboriginal English. *Jungkayi* assist the *ngimarringki* in making sure they carry out their responsibilities correctly and ensure that rules relating to access, use and treatment of that Country are followed (Bradley and Yanyuwa Families 2017: 226).

The foundation of any of this understanding is drawn from family and where family belongs, and how they belong. Men such as co-author Graham Friday Dimanyurru constantly stated that one had to know one's Dreaming links through the clan system to really know family. In 2019, in conversation with Bradley, he explained,

Table 2.1 Examples to illustrate the clan system of Yanyuwa Country, including the positioning of specific Dreaming Ancestors, the Yanyuwa authors of this book, those quoted throughout the book and those persons who are named in Old Arthur's testimony, and an illustration of how one finds all of their kin relations across the four clan group spectrum

Yanyuwa families				
Moiety A—Wabuda (fresh water)			*Moiety B—Buyuka (fire)*	
Rrumburriya		*Mambaliya-Wawukarriya*	*Wuyaliya*	*Wurdaliya*
Island Group	*Mainland Group*			
Tiger Shark	Hill Kangaroo	Brolga	Groper	Sea Turtle
White-bellied Sea Eagle	Saltwater Crocodile	Crow	Jabiru	Osprey
Dugong Hunters	File Snake	Wedge-tailed Eagle	Barracuda	Spirit People
Yanyuwa persons and their corresponding clan group				
Rrumburriya		*Mambaliya-Wawukarriya*	*Wuyaliya*	*Wurdaliya*
Island Rrumburriya				
Darby a-Muluwamara (mother of Annie a-Karrakayny		Old Isaac Walayungkuma	Saltwater Kitty a-Alanthaburra	a-Walwalmara (mother of
Jack Baju		David Isaac	Annie	Old Arthur)
Jack Buyinymanda		Birribirrikama	a-Karrakayny	Nicholas
Steve Johnston Jamarndarrka		Leanne Norman	Dinah Norman	Fitzpatrick
Mussolini Harvey		a-Wulumara	a-Marrngawi	Milyari
Keith Arthur Burrayi			Graham Friday	
Eileen McDinny			Dimanyurru	
a-Manankurrmara			Billy Miller	
Old Leo Finlay			Rijirmgu	
Mainland Rrumburriya			Emily Peter	
Old Borroloola Willy			(wife of Old	
Mundumundumara			Arthur) (Garrwa	
Old Gordon Lansen Milyindirri			Wuyaliya)	
Jilbilyijibilyi/Mundumundumara			Gadrian Hoosan	
			(Garrwa Wuyaliya)	

(continued)

Table 2.1   (continued)

Both Island/Mainland
Rrumburriya
   Lithi
   Old Arthur
   Narnungawurruwurru
   Old Banjo Didalhi
   Old Tim Timothy Rakawurlma
   Larrlya
   Pharoah – Lhawulhawu
   Mavis Timothy a-Muluwamara
   Johnson Timothy Babarramila
   Whylo McKinnon
   Philip
   Timothy Narnungawurruwurru
Human kin if EGO is Rrumburriya (and male)
EGO

Father's father	Mother's	Mother	Father's
Father's father's sister	mother's	Mother's sister	mother
Father	brother	Mother's brother	Father's
Father's sister	Mother's	Mother's brother's	mother's
Father's brother	mother	daughter	brother
Father's brother's sister		Mother's brother's	Wife
Sister		son	
Son			
Daughter			

You want to know how to get lost really quick? I will tell you, stop thinking about Dreaming. Cause, when you know that [Dreaming] you know family, you know how the rules are going to work, that's why I worry about some young people. They just throw the Dreaming away, reckon they don't need it and then…They don't know their own family…they don't know their own Country…they just lost.

A system of Law as the Yanyuwa understand it is totally dependent on family. Law is kincentric politics at work on a daily basis. To discuss family and descent lines with old people was to see a layering of time and space coming together. The centrality of familial descent reflects a particular ontology—a world patterned by intricate and dynamic networks of relations amongst people, living and dead, and between people and other forms of animate and inanimate life.

AUTHORITY, SPIRITUAL POWER AND ESSENCE

When older Yanyuwa people and specifically the Yanyuwa authors of this book would sit and speak about the Dreaming, three words would often be used: *wurrama*, *wirrimalaru* and *ngalki*. Yanyuwa Dreamings are creatures or elements that might still be found on Country, but they are also capable of acting in sentient ways. The North Wind Dreaming (*lhambiji*) is capable of thought, speech and action, possessing an abiding sentiency that is still present today. Similarly, the Groper, Whirlwind, Tiger Shark and White-Bellied Sea Eagle Dreamings—among many others—slip between a humanness and the entity that we might find situated in or moving through Yanyuwa Country day-today. All Dreamings carried *wurrama*, 'authority', an intent to travel over Country, sea and islands that allowed them to claim areas of Country for themselves. Via this authority they imbued the Country with Law—*narnu-Yuwa*—a Law that has firm judicial principles and actions associated with it.

Related to this concept of *wurrama*, 'authority', is *wirrimalaru*, 'power', or as people become more familiar with western idioms, 'spiritual power' (Kearney 2009, 2016). This is the power that still resides in the Country, at the key places where Dreamings undertook specific activities. Dreamings have *wurrama*, as do people. *Wurrama* comes from having knowledge of the Dreamings, knowledge of one's Country and the associated ceremonies and songs. *Wirrimalaru* requires constant negotiation and apprehension. In practice it involves practicing *linginmantharra*, a Yanyuwa term meaning awareness or being mindful. Negotiating wirrimalaru involves being mindful of what Country contains, where avoidance might be required, where permissions might be needed to travel, or whether certain people need to be present before actions are taken or certain Country entered. People watch such actions very carefully and make comment on any individual attempts to negotiate with these unseen forces. For example, Johnson Timothy Babarramila called out the following oration to Country as he approached a highly restricted and spiritually charged place on his mother's Country for which he was a senior *jungkayi*.

> *Wayi! Marnajingarna marni ngarna jungkayi wuwari nyuwa-ja ki-awarawu marnalu ngathangka li-malbumalbu likili-nganji ki-awarawu barni -ngalngandaya! Yuwu marnajingarna aliyaaliya jarna-wingkayi li-wankala karnalu-ngunda na-mi bawuji nya-nyngkarriya! Barni-ngalngandaya!*

—Hey! I am here the senior guardian for this place, it is my mother's Country, behind me are those old men who are paternal kin to this Country do not ignore them, do not harm them. Yes, here I am, I have not been here for a long time but the old people gave me eyes to see this place, to know this place. Listen to me! Do not pretend not to know!

In another example of how people know of and negotiate the power and Law (the quality of being *wirrimalaru*) that resides in Country, younger and mid-generation Yanyuwa will sometimes display a hesitancy around visiting places they have not been to before, or have not visited in a long time. Making sure they are in the presence of senior *jungkayi* can be one way of alleviating the worry. Leanne Norman a-Wulumara, aged at the time in her early 40s, once described her feelings about this,

> Country can be hard sometimes, closed up. Maybe its gonna do something hard to you. Cause you know them Old People [deceased elders and Ancestral Beings] when they dead they mighten give them [open access to Country], might not give us next time, if we go out hunting they won't give us anything. They might make it harder to find things and even you might get lost or sick. Those Old People might steal you away. Some of those young people, like that young girl [refers to a young woman recently held to have infringed Yanyuwa Law and gone to places she should not visit], she's young, and doesn't know who to talk to [for permission and company to visit], how to sing out, she's shy and doesn't know what she's meant to do. But she makes trouble for herself. If you don't know that Law you might just find trouble. (a-Wulumara, in Kearney 2018a: 174)

Apart from the words spoken, it is essential that such announcements are made in *wuka*—in language. Yanyuwa language is also Law; it is derived from Country and is an inheritance from the Dreaming ancestral beings. Older Yanyuwa men and women would often state that the use of language, especially on the islands and sea, the heartland of Yanyuwa Country, was a prerequisite for creating a safe place (*marakamantharra*). As Yanyuwa elder Mussolini Harvey (1994, recorded conversation with Bradley) once said, "The islands, that is the place, you gotta have language, you gotta talk proper way otherwise you don't know what might happen. Language now that's the one keeps things good, keeps Country healthy". Orations in language and the right relationships are the key to opening safe passage though places of spiritual power.

Related to these two terms *wurrama* and *wirrimalaru* is *ngalki*—perhaps the most critical word of all in beginning to understand how people hold Country, and hold their human and non-human kin. At a generic level, the most common way to translate *ngalki* is 'essence' or 'substance', but there is a deep multi-vocality to this word. From a Yanyuwa perspective, everything on their Country has its own *ngalki*, a distinguishing characteristic that grants both social and sensual agency to animate and non-animate things. At an everyday level, the scent of a flower or the smelliness of a rubbish heap is its *ngalki*; the taste of food is its *ngalki*; the tune of a song is its *ngalki*; the sound of one's own voice is *ngalki ngalki*. Every human being has their own very particular *ngalki*, which is the smell of their underarm sweat. It is at this point those words discussed above, such as 'authority' and 'power', also begin to become associated with *ngalki*. Yanyuwa Country itself is saturated with *ngalki*—the land, the sea, the islands, the reefs and the intertidal zone all have *ngalki*, drawn from the actions of the Dreamings which created them when they travelled over the Country. Dreamings imbued the Country with their *ngalki* (Bradley with Yanyuwa Families 2022; Johnson 2011; Kirton and Timothy 1977).

WUNYINGU—NAMES FROM COUNTRY

As we hope is becoming clear, Yanyuwa identity is expressed laterally through layers of meaning that tie people to place and kin. One way that individuals are tied to Country and embody a relation to it is through names derived from the Country, known as *wunyingu*—bush names. With the exception of English names, in Yanyuwa one very rarely says "My name is so and so". *Wunyingu* are names given to children by senior kin and are a kind of property; they relate people intimately to Country, Dreaming and kin. *Wunyingu* are often shared with someone of a person's paternal grandparent's generation.

Old Isaac Walayungkuma described the story of his birth, and consequently the story behind his *wunyingu*, in the following manner:

> *Wula barra nya-ngatha biyi baki rra-ngatha rra-wibi kawula-arri Wubunjawa, wundururra nya-ngatha biyilu kila-nyngkarri bardarda kararri barra ka-arri kurdandu, kilu-wunkanhu kurdandu baki kurdardi jarru barra aah wakara kilu-lhaa ardirri barra kili-nu rra-ngatha rra-wibi bardarda jiwini wurdula andaa. Kurdarrku nya-mangaji awara Wubunjawa na-mi jiwini baji, mabin barra karna-ngabu baji ambuliyalu*

bajingu karna-yanjarri, karna-arri wurdula andaa rrungku-ngatharrala
rrungku-wibila, ngarna jibiya baji, wunyatha karnilu-wundarrba
Walayungkuma, dirdikurru nya-mangaji, yiwa barra jiwini wayka rarra
mabinja, ngarna-wunyingu barranamba nya-mangaji lhuwa, ngarna-jibiya
Wubunjawa kurdardi nyungkarrku ki-awarawu, karnumba-ngka nyuwu-
mangaji ki-awarawu ngarna Walayungkuma, jibiya baji nyungku-mangaji
ki-awarala, ki-yarrambawajala, ki-kujikala, narnu-yuwa nya-mangaji.

My father and mother were camped at Wubunjawa. In the night my
father heard a baby crying. He looked everywhere he could not find any
baby, then he knew it as a spirit child and he told my mother she was going
to have a baby. Wubunjawa is Brolga Dreaming Country, the eye for the
Brolga is there, as that freshwater well, [6] I was bathing there as a spirit child
and then later I was born, my mother carried me in her womb and then I
was born. I was born from that Country, my Country, my father called me
Walayungkuma, that's the name of the olive python, that lives deep in the
well, that's my name too. I never came from any other place just Wubunjawa.
I was born from that Country. Walayungkuma is my name from that
Country, ceremony name, song name, a lot of Law in that name.

In describing the finding of his bush name, Old Isaac speaks of spirit
children, *ardirri*, which are found throughout Yanyuwa Country. The
root of the word *ardirri* is *ardu*, meaning 'child', and -*rri* is an intransitive
verb marker, but the resultant word *ardirri* is a noun, though it speaks to
the ever-present potentiality for a spirit child to be born as a human child.
Spirit children can live in lagoons, various stretches of rivers and even certain parts of the sea. Discussion of spirit child conception is a sensitive
matter, and is not done lightly. When people were moving over Country
all the time, the point at which a spirit child entered into a woman to
begin pregnancy was determined by the first faint movements of the baby
in the womb. A spirit child would enter a woman, coming from the
Country of one's father or father's father. Often the spirit child would
appear in a dream to the potential father and reveal what sex they would
be when born, and perhaps even some kind of distinguishing characteristic, such as their hair, or a bodily marker. Old men and women would
often say, *ngala ngarna ardirri karna-ngabu baji*, "when I was a spirit
child, I used to bathe there", and the comments would then be followed
by the name of a particular locality. Such a statement is also a political one,
as it is one way of stating that the individual is an owner of a particular
name and place by virtue of their spirit child source. Thus, all Yanyuwa

people can be seen as having originated through the activities of the Dreamings and the essence of the Country.

Bush names and *ardirri* identify an individual with both place and Dreamings; with a specific Dreaming and a location associated with that ancestral being. In adult life it becomes of great significance in determining the role and responsibilities which the individual has in ceremony and other related activity. As we reveal in Chap. 3, bush names are of relevance in evidencing the political rights one has to make decisions relating to Country and ceremony. *Wunyingu* affirm one's place—geographically, socially and legally—to both the individual and the broader community within the Yanyuwa lifeworld.

Linginmantharra and *Yanyuwangala*: Yanyuwa Politics as Negotiation of the Past

As these core elements of Yanyuwa ways of being demonstrate, the embodiment and enactment of Yanyuwa Law is a sophisticated negotiation of time and the beginnings of Country. Retelling and reinscribing the Law and social memory which holds it is referred to in Yanyuwa as *linginmantharra*, an intransitive verb meaning remembering and being mindful (Bradley and Johnson 2015: 5). The prefix *lingi-* is a term unto itself used to describe people or animals as highly intelligent or keen of hearing, two qualities which are closely related in a Yanyuwa ontology and a semantic link which speaks to the importance of being capable of truly hearing and enacting something in oral traditions more broadly (Bradley 1997: 242–3). The verbal suffix *-mantharra* infers the practices of remembering, recalling and retelling and being mindful and attentive (Bradley and Yanyuwa Families 2016: 277). In a Yanyuwa sense, and contrary to western logic, old people and Dreamings who inhabited the Country in the past are spoken of as *li-ambirriju*—'being in front', or 'those who are in the lead'—and that one maintains their place in the contemporary world by looking 'forward' to the old people (Bradley with Yanyuwa Families 2022). There is an important sense of Yanyuwa Law having been left by those in front for *li-wumbijingu*—'those in the middle' as the present generation of elders—and *li-ngulakarringu*—'those who come behind' as the next generation who it is hoped will be knowledgeable Law people (Bradley 1997: 22, Bradley with Yanyuwa Families 2022).

Li-ardubirri jalini li-ngulakaringu, nganu li-wurrirri li-wumbijingu alu li-wankala li-ngabangaku li-ambirriju.
—The children are behind, we adult people are in the middle and the old people, the deceased ones, are in the front. (Bradley and Yanyuwa Families 2016: 424)

For Yanyuwa, the negotiation of the past is not only socially expressive but also inherently political. The practice of *linginmantharra* is in a broader sense the real substance of *narnu-Yuwa*; the Yanyuwa Law which holds the kincentric relationships that tie everything and everyone on Country together (Bradley and Yanyuwa Families 2016: 385). This way of negotiating the past involves powerful claims to political authority—that is, to apprehend the contemporary and future consequences of past events, actions and experiences in accordance with Yanyuwa Law.

This negotiation of the past can be said to be at the heart of *Yanyuwangala*—a term used to describe a Yanyuwa way of being, knowing and inhabiting Country. *Yanyuwangala* is perhaps also the Yanyuwa word for epistemology. In contemporary times *Yanyuwangala* is spoken of as a direct contrast with *Munangangala*, a western way of being and inhabiting place.

Yarrambawaja—Ceremony

Yarrambawaja is the Yanyuwa word for ceremony and ritual. It is fundamental in both carrying out and implementing the Law, as well as passing the Law on from senior kin to younger generations. Political authority is derived from *narnu-nyirrka*, an authorised ceremonial space where social and political authority is revealed and enacted, and where the Country is 'held up'. Senior Yanyuwa kin such as Mussolini Harvey and Annie a-Karrakayny, who were also knowledgeable about western legal systems, described *yarrambawaja* as 'like a parliament'; everything is decided there and the Law is seen and heard. Everyone goes away 'clear' in the knowledge of where they belong, where others belong in relation to them and the basis of this knowledge in Law.

Yarrambawaja is the praxis of Yanyuwa Law, where kin and Country are ritually 'straightened out' and brought into lawful relation with one another through performance, ceremonial roles, obligations and the display of knowledge. Ceremonies are sites of authority from which people can say they belong to clan and Country, or are kin to a specific Dreaming or non-human phenomena. *Yarrambawaja* reinforces and enacts these relationships between kin and Country, and in this sense, there is little binary between kin and Country in this field of *yarrambawaja*; each lives within the other.

There are many different Yanyuwa ceremonies; each relating to distinct elements of Yanyuwa Law and belonging to the four clan groups which organise Yanyuwa Country and Law (Bradley 2010). *Yarrambawaja* requires the participation of *li-wirdiwalangu*, those with the authority in relation to each ceremony to teach and empower people with knowledge. Senior kin are considered those responsible for holding and leading ceremonies belonging to them. Yanyuwa ceremonial performance strengthens the health of Country, facilitates the departure of deceased kin back into Country, initiates young boys into manhood and enlivens and reinstates clan relationships. Another form of ritual practice to support Law are *kujika*, a form of song poetry that runs through Yanyuwa Country. These are a preeminent form and expression of Law.

Kujika—Songlines

Kujika is the Yanyuwa word for 'songlines'. *Kujika* are sung by men during ceremonial performances. In this way, the ceremonial praxis of *yarrambawaja* is predicated on *kujika*. Dinah Norman a-Marrngawi describes the relationship between *kujika* and *yarrambawaja* in the following terms: "the ceremony (*yarrmbawaja*) sits on the surface, we see it, we dance it, but the *kujika* is deep below in the earth, it is the *kujika* that holds everything" (Bradley with Yanyuwa Families 2022: 96).

Kujika tell of the journeys and actions of the Dreamings as they crisscrossed the Country interacting with one another: marking, naming and shaping the Yanyuwa world. Each *kujika* consists of hundreds of verses. The language of *kujika* is not the same version of Yanyuwa that is spoken on a day-to-day basis. While the occasional word is recognisable, the words of these songs are an archaic form of Yanyuwa called *wuka ki-yijandu*, the 'language from the Dreaming', or *ambuliyanynguwarra wuka*, the 'most ancient or oldest language'. As a result, translating *kujika* is an exceptionally difficult task (see Bradley and Yanyuwa Families 2022; Bradley 2010). Given their intertwined existence in practice, *yarrambawaja* and *kujika* share some fundamental features. Each *kujika* belongs to one of the four Yanyuwa clans. Like Country and Dreamings, each *kujika* has both *ngimirringki* who 'own' it through their father's kin and *jungkayi* who are 'guardians' for it through their mother's kin. *Kujika* can be public or secret in nature, though context is needed to determine which ceremony in which it will be performed (see also Bradley with Yanyuwa Families 2022; Bradley 2010).

A *kujika* follows the *a-yabala* (path, or road) of a specific ancestral being through the land. When Yanyuwa people sing *kujika*, they are *wandayarra a-yabala*—following the path or road of the *kujika*. Just as Yanyuwa people speak about Dreamings as enduring presences and agents on Country, there is an understanding that these songs continue to resonate through the Country; *ja-wingkayi ki-awarala* (it is running in the Country). Just as the Dreamings are spoken to on an everyday basis in the present tense, so too *kujika* and their movements through the Country are only spoken of in the present tense, never in the past or future tense verbs. Thus, songlines are 'running', 'moving', 'flowing', 'rising up' and 'descending', always in the present, and following very precise paths. The following quote by Old Isaac Walayungkuma is a common way of expressing knowledge of songlines.

> *Kujika nya-ngantha jiwini marnajingulaji jiwini mulungka ngathangka barra*
> —The songline is here at this place right now, it is with me in my mouth.

The singing of *kujika* is a collective undertaking. People gather in ceremonial performance to sing together and to reinforce the value of the song and the Law that resides in Country. It is men who sing *kujika*, but women listen too, and know the *kujika*; it is their Law, too. Women also have their own songlines called *nanda-wangirli*. The songlines sung by women primarily concern the travels of groups of Women Dreamings called *a-Mararabarna* and are a celebration and reminder of the collective responsibility that women have to their Country. They are sung at the initiation ceremonies of young men and were once sung at their own restricted ceremonies. Such songs serve the same purpose as *kujika* sung by the men.

Everything that is outlined above comes to the foreground in a discussion of Country, whether this be amongst Yanyuwa families themselves or as is often the case in contemporary times with mining companies, environmental managers, town and heritage planners and various Indigenous organisational representatives who work under Federal, State and Territory legislation to assist Indigenous peoples in the management of their lands.

Of key concern, for Yanyuwa, at these meetings is that the right people under Yanyuwa Law speak for the Country in question and that a general collective consensus can be reached.

COLLECTIVE DECISION-MAKING: YANYUWA PROCESSES OF REACHING CONSENSUS

In Yanyuwa, decision-making can be summed up by the phrase *kalinyamba-wukalwukanyi mindibirrinja awara*, which translates as "they would talk and talk to each other, until everything was settled and agreed upon". This phrase reflects a process of coming together to work through conflicts and decisions with the aim of reaching consensus and agreement among senior kin. The underlying principle which always informs decision-making and any effort of agreement-making is that of family (*li-malarnngu*); it is people's concern for family that increases a sense of loyalty and group care for one another. In Chap. 3, we present an account of Law which is told through oral testimony. This example demonstrates how key individuals within the Yanyuwa community would make collectively agreed-upon decisions, in alignment with the practice and continuation of Law.

In a forum where consensus must be reached, for example, in instances when mining exploration licences over Yanyuwa Country are being applied for or when royalty distributions are being discussed, communication is often subtle. Collective experience and knowledge enable greater depth of understanding as to each person's perspectives, interests or intentions. Compared to western ways of seeking consensus, verbal communication for Yanyuwa is somewhat 'quieter' as everyone is known; everyone is emplaced and there are no strangers. Yanyuwa people describe success in arriving at a consensus as *ngambala wiji*—"all of us without separation". In a Yanyuwa sense the stomach is the seat of emotions, feelings or desires, and another phrase that people would use after coming to a consensus decision is *kambala-yabirri ngambala-wurdu*—"we are all with goodness in our stomach", which in effect conveys that "we are all content with what has transpired". These terms demonstrate that in Yanyuwa decision-making, it is the norm for members of the group to feel satisfied in a mutual resolve before any actions take place. To leave such meetings without any sense of consensus paves the way for intense family politicking and arguments, and this can lead to *budijbudij awara*—"a confused and entangled Country".

In the ebb and flow of life in the remote community of Borroloola, there is a sense of duty and emotional care for each person's well-being. Close individual and family relationships scaffold group discussion of issues facing the community, and care is taken to diffuse friction. This isn't to suggest there are not occasions where hard words are spoken or difficult decisions are made by individuals who have the authority to make them. Whatever the circumstances, it is in this forum of collective decision-making where one sees the prominence and leadership of *li-wirdiwalangu*—the people who have authority. Senior kin and elders may hold greater sway than others when coming together to discuss matters of Law. Nevertheless, a Yanyuwa way of coming to consensus is achieved by nurturing individuals and explaining things to one another, not a tough approach which demands obedience.

ORALITY AND TRANSMISSION OF LAW

Yanyuwa kinship, politics, song, poetry and narratives are all associated with place, with Country, as inclusive of the land and sea of the southwest Gulf of Carpentaria. Yanyuwa is a firmly emplaced language of oral traditions rooted in time and place and in the person who was or is still speaking it. It is imperative to understand that the Law we have outlined here was shaped by a language other than the one we are now writing in (see Bradley 2020). Yanyuwa Law is informed by rules and ways of knowing that western texts and books have never known. In Yanyuwa, the term for language is *wuka*, and to understand and speak *wuka* is a powerful claim to know something; authority in this knowledge lies in the language itself. We cannot expect Yanyuwa knowledge to be translated and remediated in western terms without betrayal or miscomprehension. For those who meet these knowledges from a western way of seeing and being, there is often the need to develop new habits of mind in order to understand (Kearney 2020, 2021). The knowledges we have thus far presented here have slipped from the oral to the textual, at the expense of transmitting an understanding of the land, sea and people who have brought these texts into being (Bradley 2020). The singers and tellers of these knowledges are the recorders and holders of them in their true sense, not the translator or linguist whose secondary tongue and ears remediate them.

In a Yanyuwa way of knowing all stories and songs associated with Law are addressed to a group of human beings that have ears to hear without translation. They are spoken and sung in the knowledge that recently or long-since deceased kin and non-human kin such, dugong, sea eagles and sharks are listening. Any shift from an oral tradition to a written culture will affect the functioning of memory and transmission to old people and non-human listeners. It affects the meanings that are given to the words; it affects the meaning of the language itself and calls into question debates of worth ´and value in relation to still being able to tie knowledge to Country. The printed word becomes an abstraction, whereas the full force of an oral tradition is always clear and it does in the end affect the meaning of meaning.

An oral tradition is not just learned and transmitted through memorisation. For people functioning within a tradition of orality, the various forms of song, poetry or oratory of speech are seen as the highest form of the language. Language is acquired through an open-ended gathering of vocabulary and knowledge along with the grammar and social rules that enable these elements to assemble in ever more complex and self-integrated ways (see Bradley and Yanyuwa Families 2017, Bradley with Yanyuwa Families 2022) To retell an event based purely upon memory may preserve a particular form, but its growth and development has been halted, and its audience is largely irrelevant. The full functioning of an oral tradition is rather more like a journey, not just something to be repeated on demand. Of course, memory is essential to the process, but it is not the essential means by which it works.

Old Yanyuwa men in the late twentieth century could sing their Law, including the hundreds of verses of songlines that traversed many kilometres of mainland, islands and sea, thus creating a geography of sound. An oral tradition is always more than just what is being heard. In the orality held by these old men, there is the journey of the self; of the people singing, of the intersubjective commentary with place and ancestry. Thus, by listening one enters a doorway that leads into other worlds that live beside and behind, or perhaps in front of our own. The learning of such songs and the worlds and words of Law that surround them is not about rote acquisition, but rather it is the experience that leads to the knowing, the participation in the practice and praxis that bind them. When the experience occurs, then the knowledge is digested, and in order for the experience to occur then the story must unfold within the freedom of the tradition that holds it.

Indigenous languages such as Yanyuwa and their orality are the sound of an authoritative link to the land. As the orality of the stories which convey and support Law are lost, their performative character is also forfeited as well as their links to Country. For many generations of Yanyuwa families, it has been orality that has held Country, but increasingly the printed word (often in English) has come to dominate. In this process the subtle nuances of meaning can be lost, for there are words that defy a direct translation into English, and the politics of speech are no longer accorded the place they once were. Country then becomes stripped of the particularising stories that hold it. As any continued loss of orality and oral tradition occurs, the felt primacy of places are forgotten and superseded by an abstraction called 'space'. In a Yanyuwa way of thinking, this creates a dreadfully flat ontology, a homogenous and placeless void (Kearney 2021).

If the language of the Country is no longer voiced, places become incidental, arbitrary backdrops for human events that could nearly have happened anywhere. As the technology of writing spreads through an oral culture, it removes the palpable power and personality of particular places which can begin to fade. A story once so tied to place in an oral tradition can be carried away and stored; the document becomes separated from the place to which the words were once so intimately tied. This very act of writing down such a place-based world renders knowledge and people separable from actual places. The stories become independent of locale, and the Country, in turn, becomes remote and unfettered; the multiple commentaries and angles of perception that also existed in relation to the words are not there.

Over the last 40 years the rate of change at Borroloola has been rapid and at times beyond the control of Yanyuwa people and the Law to be active participants or even discussants (see Johnson 2011). These changes exist at many levels in regard to land and sea use, mining, education and health. The most telling indicator of the rapidity of socio-cultural change in Borroloola is the dwindling number of speakers of Yanyuwa language. In 1980 there were approximately 260 people who had a full working grasp of the Yanyuwa language and its gendered dialects. In 2022, there are only four such speakers of Yanyuwa. Yanyuwa families are deeply aware of the ramifications of these changes, and while there is deep sadness in the face of these rapid shifts in the Yanyuwa lifeworld, there is also a growing resilience among Yanyuwa families in navigating these changes.

ASPECTS OF CHANGE: CULTURAL SHIFTS AND GENERATIONAL NUANCE

The Yanyuwa men and women who have contributed to and co-authored this book have always demonstrated a commitment to 'strong Law'. According to Yanyuwa, strong Law is expressed in language and through knowledge of the ceremonial activity which places clan groups and individuals into particular relationships with one another and their Country. For elders, strong Law is now deemed vulnerable (see Adgemis 2017). When John Bradley first moved to Borroloola in 1980 and began his career-long collaboration with Yanyuwa families, Yanyuwa language was the dominant form of communication, and, when anthropologist John Avery (1988: 9) undertook ethnography with Yanyuwa in the late 1970s till the mid 1980s, ceremony continued to be the 'apex of law'. The dramatic change in lifestyles as Yanyuwa families became centralised to the township of Borroloola in the late 1950s has also had implications for the transmission of Law (Adgemis 2017; Kearney 2009, 2014).

As many middle-aged Yanyuwa men went to work at cattle stations over long periods of time from the 1930s through to the 1980s, they often spent the lions' share of each year away from Borroloola. This meant that many ceremonial and cultural practices, and the intergenerational transfer of knowledge that naturally accompanies cultural praxis, were disrupted. By the early 1990s the last of the great ceremonies were no longer being performed. By the early 2000s, only one of the many Yanyuwa *kujika* (songlines) which were once known was being sung. In 2022, this single *kujika* is still remembered and allows for *a-marndiwa* initiation ceremonies to be held so that young boys may still be initiated into manhood. As a result, this initiation ceremony is the only ceremony younger generations of Yanyuwa have seen performed regularly within their community (see Adgemis 2017; Johnson 2011: 256). Senior Yanyuwa men and women, including co-authors of this book, knew that this decline in language, song and ceremony would unfold, and are acutely aware of the challenges they face in teaching Law to younger generations.

> You know I followed my father all my life and my mother, and now they are gone, but we still have to think about the Law they left for us, and you know I worry about my son and grandson, so I think all the time what do we do?
> —Mavis Timothy a-Muluwaramara

There are times at night when I am sitting quietly by myself and I look at my sleeping grandchildren and I think of all the things that they will never know. They will never see the great and sacred ceremonies or hear the songs of the old people. —Dinah Norman a-Marrngawi (Bradley 2010: xv)

You know we got to work really hard at this, we got to give these young people an idea, how that Law can hold them, make them strong, give them ears to hear, you know, to know how family and Dreaming work, that's the main thing and then how Dreaming work for song and ceremony. —Graham Friday Dimanyurru

In spite of rapid changes, younger generations continue to be active in attempting to learn aspects of Law and what their old people know of their ancestral homelands (Adgemis 2017; Kearney 2018a, b; Kearney and Kowalewski 2017). However there are tensions among younger Yanyuwa men and women that come from being the new wave of living repositories for continuing Yanyuwa identity in a context characterised by rapid change and competing influences, as well as the ironic dissonance of increased currency of links to the past in a setting where there is less opportunity to actually practise using them. A Yanyuwa sense of self in relation to Country and family—at the core of a particular localised sense of well-being—challenges what most people in western society can ever truly empathise with. Yet ongoing Yanyuwa resilience today is demonstrated by the fact that younger Yanyuwa people carry the legacy of their ancestors, all the while engaging with it and adapting it as best they can and see fit, relative to what lies ahead of them.

Yanyuwa responses to change and exclusion from debate about the value of their Law in Australia are vividly on display through their choice to become involved in one of the first ever land rights claims in Australia, under the *Aboriginal Land Rights Act (Northern Territory) 1976* (Australian Government 1976). Yanyuwa began this process in 1975, activating their right to seek legal redress to the colonial theft of their lands and waters, in accordance with Commonwealth land rights legislation (Avery 2016). The first claim, heard in 1976, which led to the partial return of ancestral lands and waters, was followed by a reclaim in 1992 for unreturned lands and waters (Bradley 1992). The reclaim was successful and resulted in Yanyuwa having nearly all of their island Country returned and given the status of Aboriginal freehold title, to the exclusion of all others (see Kearney 2018a, b, Kearney 2022). In 2000 the community once again mobilised the *Aboriginal Land Rights Act (Northern Territory) 1976* to claim back their intertidal sea Country, including the sea grass beds and river banks. This was to ensure a full return of Aboriginal ownership to parts of Country that are home to important species such as dugongs and sea turtles. This case remains unresolved (meaning a final approval and ratification of the legal decision has not been yet delivered), despite the Land Commissioner reaching a determination in favour of Aboriginal title.

Yanyuwa men and women have also engaged with various forms of media and creative expression to tell their stories and to share aspects of their Law in an effort to keep it vital and strong, such as the films *Kanymarda Yuwa*, Two Laws (Borroloola Aboriginal Community 1981); *Buwarrala Akarriya*, Journey East (Yanyuwa Community 1989); *Ka-Wawayawayama*, Aeroplane Dance (Borroloola Aboriginal Community 1992); and *Buwarrala Aryah*, Journey West (Borroloola Aboriginal Community 2019). They have collaborated with animators to tell important narratives of Law associated with their Country, in the form of multi-modal digital animations of Country and the Dreaming.[7] And they have worked with academics and authors to develop texts that speak to the Law that holds their Country, including an atlas of Yanyuwa Country called *Forget About Flinders* (Yanyuwa Families et al. 2003) and a recent book on their rock art and maritime culture, *Jakardu Wuka—Too many stories: Narratives of rock art from Yanyuwa Country* (li-Yanyuwa li-Wirdiwalangu Elders Group et al. forthcoming 2023).

In the face of great change, Yanyuwa men and women have been tireless in demonstrating the importance of their knowledge and the need for their Law. They have not been passive in the face of over 230 years of coloniality. This text too is part of an active response to change and a commitment to sharing and safeguarding Law.

CHAPTER OVERVIEW

There are two domains that still take precedence in Yanyuwa thought when matters of Law are discussed: family and Country. Interactions between kin and the physicality of the land and sea that make up Country require daily mediation. This is Law in process. Once these relationships were regularly, deliberately and dramatically expressed through ceremony, where performance and song materially enacted and renewed these associations. The performance of Law as derived from the Dreamings and expressed through political relationships of owners (*ngimirringki*) and managers (*jungkayi*) was and remains the ideological underpinning of holding Country. In the time of ceremony, the Law was demonstrated to be a binding power. Even today, in the liminal space, devoid of the praxis of ceremony, the Law is still a force and body of knowledge that allows for remembrance and continuity in regard to family and Country. Today, Law is expressed most substantially through human relationships and connections between families and parts of Country over which people travel and hunt.

The Law should never be seen as a body of codified knowledge, or a finite system which a single person can 'know' everything. Rather, Law should be understood as being differentially distributed across the population according to age, gender, kinship, clans and Country. All of these elements work together to determine who might have knowledge of aspects of the Law. A critical qualification for access to this knowledge is descent, experience and, at times, residence and participation in the increasingly vexed realms of everyday community politics, land and resource rights and native title.[8] People speak for their own particular place, which means that each person, is entitled to distinctive portions and perspectives of the Law.

As the story we share in the next chapter illustrates, the loss of knowledge and language between generations over many years of colonial disturbance and rapid change has led to real challenges in carrying Yanyuwa Law forward. Younger generations face a challenge in putting the Law as the old people knew it into practice in the twenty-first century, while simultaneously establishing their own cultural identities as saltwater Yanyuwa people in a world their ancestors would scarcely recognise. It is hoped that by sharing this story of Law, there is an opportunity for a diverse audience of readers, including future generations of Yanyuwa themselves, to gain an insight into the realpolitik of Yanyuwa knowledge and how Law operates to stabilise and strengthen this community.

NOTES

1. Outstations are autonomous, often self-established settlements where Aboriginal people live in small family groups away from town. The outstation movement or homeland movement refers to the voluntary relocation of Aboriginal people from towns to these locations.

2. The expression 'old people' is frequently adopted by Yanyuwa. In this particular instance it is referring to deceased kin. But it can also mean current-day elders, deceased kin or ancestral beings. Context will most often determine the manner in which the terms is being used. County is said to be alive with the presence of old people, in this case, referring to both the spirits of deceased kin and also the ancestral beings which came with the Dreaming and moved through Country, creating its features.

3. This process of decision-making mapped out over a long period of time, as elders came to terms with elements of change within their community. This became most evident throughout the 1960s and throughout the 1980s.

4. Yanyuwa has two distinct dialects for men and women. In the above example *na-Yuwa* is men's speech and *ni-Yuwa* is women's speech (see Yanyuwa Families and Bradley 2016, 2017; Gaby and Bradley 2020).

5. Dreamings and the spirits of deceased kin are often referred to in Aboriginal English as 'old people', or in Yanyuwa as *li-wankala*.

6. As the Dreamings travelled over Yanyuwa Country they sometimes left their eyes. The eyes became transformed into freshwater wells. They are often an important site of Dreaming Ancestral power and a source for *ardirri*. People can talk of bathing is these wells before being born. "*Karna-ngabu baji Minyadawiji baku barra baku karna-yanjarri*" "I bathed in the waters of the well at the place called Minyadawiji, and then much later I was born" (see also Bradley with Yanyuwa Families 2022: 50–51).

7. The *Wunungu Awara: Animating Indigenous Knowledges* project is hosted by Monash University and led by John Bradley. The Yanyuwa animations can be accessed at http://artsonline.monash.edu.au/Countrylines-archive/.

8. Native Title is governed by the Native Title Act 1993 (Commonwealth of Australia). It is the legislative recognition that Aboriginal and Torres Strait Islander people have rights and interests to land and waters according to their traditional law and customs as set out in Australian Law.

References

Adgemis, P. 2017. *We Are Yanyuwa – No Matter What: Town Life, Family and Change*. PhD Thesis, Monash University, Australia.

Australian Government. 1976. *Aboriginal Land Rights (Northern Territory) Act 1976*, No. 191, 1976. Available at https://www.legislation.gov.au/Details/C2019C00117

Avery, J. 1988. *The Law People: History, Society and Initiation in the Borroloola Area of the Northern Territory*. PhD Thesis, University of Sydney, Australia.

Avery, J. 2016. Borroloola: The first land claim. *Land Rights News, Northern Edition*, July 2016. Available at: https://www.nlc.org.au/uploads/pdfs/LRN_July-2016_Web.pdf

Avery, J., and McLaughlin, D. 1977. *Submission by Northern Land Council to the Aboriginal Land Commissioner on the Borroloola Region Land Claim.* Darwin: Northern Land Council.

Baker, R. 1989. *Land is Life: Continuity Through Change for the Yanyuwa from the Northern Territory of Australia.* PhD Thesis, University of Adelaide, Australia.

Baker, R. 1990. Coming In? The Yanyuwa as a case study in the geography of contact history. *Aboriginal History* 14(1/2): 25–60.

Baker, R. 1999. *Land is Life: Continuity Through Change for the Yanyuwa from the Northern Territory of Australia.* Sydney: Allen and Unwin.

Borroloola Aboriginal Community. 1981. *Kanymarda Yuwa* – Two Laws [film]. Directed and produced by Carolyn Strachan and Alessandro Cavadini. Red Dirt Films and the Australian Film Commission.

Borroloola Aboriginal Community. 1992. *Ka-wayawayama* – Aeroplane Dance [film]. Directed and produced by Trevor Graham. Film Australia.

Borroloola Aboriginal Community. 2019. *Buwarrala Aryah* – Journey West [film]. Directed by Gadrian Jarwijalmar Hoosan, produced by Jason De Santolo, Mandy King and Fabio Cavadini. Ronin Films, Australia.

Bowern, C. (Ed.). 2022. *The Oxford Guide to Australian Languages.* Oxford: Oxford University Press.

Bradley, J. 1988. *Yanyuwa Country.* Melbourne: Greenhouse Publishing.

Bradley, J. 1992. *Warnarrwarnarr-Barranyi Land Claim.* Darwin: Northern Land Council.

Bradley, J. 1997. *Li-Anthawirriyarra, People of the Sea: Yanyuwa Relations with Their Maritime Environment.* Ph.D. thesis, Northern Territory University, Australia.

Bradley, J. 2008. Singing through the sea: Song, sea and emotion. In S. Shaw and A. Francis (Eds.) *Deep Blue: Critical Reflections on Nature, Religion and Water.* Abingdon, Oxon: Routledge, pp. 17–32.

Bradley, J. 2010. *Singing Saltwater Country.* Sydney: Allen & Unwin.

Bradley, J. 2020. Writing from the edge: Writing what was never meant to be written. A. Kearney and J. Bradley (Eds.) *Reflexive Ethnographic Practice: Three Generations of Social Researchers in One Place.* New York: Palgrave Macmillan, pp. 39–64.

Bradley, J., with Yanyuwa Families. 2022. *It's Coming from the Times in Front of Us: Country, Kin and the Dugong Hunter Songline.* Melbourne, Victoria: Australian Scholarly Publishing.

Bradley, J., and Yanyuwa Families. 2017. *Wuka nya- nganunga li- Yanyuwa li-Anthawirriyarra: Language for Us, the Yanyuwa Saltwater People* (Vol 2). Melbourne, VIC: Australian Scholarly Publishing.

Bradley, J., and Johnson, S. 2015. 'Those old men who sing are our professors': Songlines, esoteric knowledge or empirical data'. *UNESCO Observatory Journal: Multi-Disciplinary Research in the Arts* 4(2): 1–23.

Bradley, J., and Yanyuwa Families 2016. *Wuka nya- nganunga li- Yanyuwa li-Anthawirriyarra: Language for Us, the Yanyuwa Saltwater People* (Vol 1). Melbourne, VIC: Australian Scholarly Publishing.

Commonwealth of Australia. Native Title Act 1993, No.110. Available at: https://www.legislation.gov.au/Details/C2019C00054

Gaby, A., and Bradley, J. 2020. Wulaya 'head' in Yanyuwa. In I. Kraska-Szlenk (Ed.) *Embodiment in Cross-Linguistic Studies: The "Head"*. Leiden, The Netherlands: Brill, pp. 263–272.

Johnson, S. 2011. *Barra Bawuji Marrirru, Lhaba Anywaumaya, Stop! Be Quiet! Listen to Country!* PhD thesis, University of Queensland, Australia.

Kearney, A. 2009. *Before the Old People and Still Today: Yanyuwa Places and Narratives of Engagement*. Melbourne: Australian Scholarly Publishing.

Kearney, A. 2014. *Cultural Wounding, Healing and Emerging Ethnicities*. New York: Palgrave Macmillan.

Kearney, A. 2016. Cultural wounding and healing: Change as ongoing cultural production in a remote Indigenous Australian community. In T. Hylland Eriksen and E. Schober (Eds.) *Identity Destabilized: Living in an Overheated World*. Chicago: University of Chicago Press, pp. 114–134.

Kearney, A. 2018a. Intimacy and distance: Indigenous relationships to country in northern Australia. *Ethnos* 83(1): 172–191. https://doi.org/10.108 0/00141844.2016.1236827

Kearney, A. 2018b. Returning to that which was never lost: Indigenous Australian saltwater identities, a history of Australian land claims and the paradox of return. *History and Anthropology* 29(2): 184–203. https://doi.org/10.108 0/02757206.2017.1397646

Kearney, A. 2019. Interculturalism and responsive reflexivity in a settler colonial context. *Religions* 10: 199. Available at: https://www.mdpi.com/2077-1444/10/3/199, https://doi.org/10.3390/rel10030199

Kearney, A. 2020. Mobility of mind: Can we change our epistemic habit through sustained ethnographic encounters? In A. Kearney and J. Bradley (Eds.) *Reflexive Ethnographic Practice: Three Generations of Social Researchers in One Place*. New York: Palgrave Macmillan, pp. 65–94.

Kearney, A. 2021. *Keeping Company: An Anthropology of Being-In-Relation*. London: Routledge.

Kearney, A. 2022. 'The law has changed, and you can get some of your land back…': Aboriginal land rights, subjection and the law. In P. Cane, L. Ford, and M. McMillan (Eds.) *The Cambridge Legal History of Australia*. Cambridge: Cambridge University Press, pp. 354–376.

Kearney, A., and Bradley, J. 2015. When a long way in a bark canoe becomes a quick trip in a boat: Changing relationships to sea country & Yanyuwa watercraft technology. *Quaternary International* 385: 166–176. https://doi.org/10.1016/j.quaint.2014.07.004

Kearney, A., and Kowalewski, G. 2017. Refuting timelessness: Emerging relationships to intangible cultural heritage for younger Indigenous Australians. In M. Stefano and P. Davis (Eds.) *The Routledge Companion to Intangible Cultural Heritage*. Abingdon, Oxon: Routledge, pp. 285–299.

Kirton, J., and Timothy, N. 1977. Yanyuwa concepts relating to 'skin'. *Oceania* 47(4): 320–322.

li-Yanyuwa li-Wirdiwalangu Elders Group, Brady, L., Bradley, J., and Kearney, A. Forthcoming 2023. *Jakardu Wuka – Too many Stories: Narratives of Rock Art from Yanyuwa Country in Northern Australia's Gulf of Carpentaria*. Sydney: University of Sydney Press.

Reay, M. 1962. Subsections at Borroloola. *Oceania* 33(2): 90–115.

Reay, M. 1970. A decision as narrative. In R. M. Berndt (Ed.) *Australian Aboriginal Anthropology*. Perth, WA: Australian Institute of Aboriginal Studies: pp. 164–173.

Roberts, T. 2005. *Frontier Justice: A History of the Gulf Country to 1900*. St Lucia, Australia: University of Queensland Press.

Salmón, E. 2000. Kincentric ecology. *Ecological Applications* 10(5): 1327–1332. https://doi.org/10.1890/1051-0761(2000)010[1327:KEIPOT]2.0.CO;2

Senos, R., Lake, F., Turner, N., and Martinez, D. 2006. Traditional ecological knowledge and restoration practice. In D. Apostal, M. Sinclair, and E. Higgs (Eds.) *Restoring the Pacific Northwest: The Art and Science of Ecological Restoration in Cascadia*. Washington, DC: Island, pp. 393–402.

Trigger, D. 1992. *Whitefella Comin': Aboriginal Responses to Colonialism in Northern Australia*. New York: Cambridge University Press.

Yanyuwa Community. 1989. *Buwarrala Akarriya* - Journey East [film]. Directed and produced by Debbie Sonnenberg. Marndaa Productions.

Yanyuwa Families, Bradley, J., and Cameron, N. 2003. *Forget About Flinders: An Indigenous Atlas of the Southwest Gulf of Carpentaria*. Canberra, NSW: Australian Institute of Aboriginal Studies.

CHAPTER 3

Testimonies of Yanyuwa Law and Kincentric Order

Abstract In this chapter we present a demonstration of Indigenous Law in practice at a local level, a detailed account of an oral testimony given by Yanyuwa elder Old Arthur Narnungawurruwurru (Old Arthur). This example demonstrates how key individuals within the Yanyuwa community would come together to make collectively agreed-upon decisions, in alignment with the practice and continuation of Law. The story as outlined in this chapter was shared with one of the authors (Bradley) by Old Arthur himself, at the request of his niece, and co-author Annie a-Karrakayny, a senior Yanyuwa Law woman. The testimony relates to matters of the Dreaming, kinship, succession, land and sea rights and political decision-making processes. In the first part of this chapter, we present this account of Law piece by piece, first in Yanyuwa language and then in translated English.

This chapter shows the many ways in which Law has complexity. This is a vision of Indigenous cultures and their Laws as highly adept at accommodating, resisting and negotiating internal pressures, but even more so the external pressures that distinguish settler colonial and Indigenous relations.

Keywords Yanyuwa • Oral testimony • Practicing Law • Kincentric • Land Rights • Orality

© The Author(s) 2023   65
A. Kearney et al., *Indigenous Law and the Politics of Kincentricity and Orality*, https://doi.org/10.1007/978-3-031-19239-5_3

In this chapter we present a demonstration of Indigenous Law in practice at a local level, a detailed account of an oral testimony given by Yanyuwa elder Old Arthur Narnungawurruwurru (Old Arthur). This was shared with one of the authors (Bradley) by Old Arthur himself, at the request of his niece, and co-author Annie a-Karrakayny, a senior Yanyuwa Law woman and her classificatory mother's brother Old Tim Timothy Rakawurlma (Old Tim Rakawurlma). Old Arthur was Annie's 'full' mother's brother (*kardirdi*) (that is, her mother and Old Arthur were direct siblings, by blood), an important relationship often linked to the sharing of knowledge and mentoring in Law. This occurred as part of the process of Old Arthur explaining and stating his rights to, and political oversight for, particular parts of Yanyuwa Country. The testimony relates to matters of the Dreaming, kinship, succession, land and sea rights and political decision-making processes. In the first part of this chapter, we present this account of Law piece by piece, first in Yanyuwa language and then in translated English.

In the second part of the chapter, we engage with a retelling of this oral testimony by a younger Yanyuwa man Philip Timothy Narnungawurruwurru in 2000. This occurred in the context of a land claim under the *Aboriginal Land Rights (Northern Territory) Act 1976* (Australian Government 1976), again at the urging of Annie a-Karrakayny (who Philip called *ardiyardi*—niece). Confronted with having to provide evidence to the Federal Court of Australia in the course of this legislative land claim, Philip had the responsibility to retell Old Arthur's story in order to reinforce continuing relationships, and to perform a public and political act aimed at asserting his, and more broadly Yanyuwa, kincentric rights to Country. This event was stressful and stands to illustrate the tensions that often exist between Indigenous Law and western law. This case demonstrates that Australian Commonwealth Law stands to challenge matters of orality and thus the legitimacy and maintenance of Indigenous Law (Kearney 2022). The event of a land claim compels a deeper discussion of the communal pressures and challenges which emerge over time for Indigenous practitioners of Law.

Old Arthur was Phillip's classificatory paternal grandfather—*murimuri*, a formal kinship term given to the older brothers of one's actual or classificatory paternal grandfather. These two men shared a *wunyingu*—bush name, Narnungawurruwurru,[1] and both were of the Rrumburriya clan and thus shared Law. Let us start by painting a picture of Old Arthur's life and, drawing on the explanation of Yanyuwa kinship and Country presented in the previous chapter, explain the socio-cultural context in which he told this account of the Law.

OLD ARTHUR NARNUNGAWURRUWURRU

Old Arthur Narnungawurruwurru was born on Vanderlin Island in the early 1900s (see Fig. 3.1). His father Lithi was the senior *ngimirringki* for North Island, Centre Island, Skull Island and the Black and White Craggy Islands. This group of islands and sea Country are known by the overarching name of Barranyi. Old Arthur's *ardirri* (spirit child) came from Winalamba, a very important site on the central west coast of North Island. Oral tradition speaks of his father Lithi being called *Bujarinja* (the Bushranger) because he never came into the township of Borroloola; he remained on the islands, despite the colonial pressures to relocate. Lithi's canoe was called *a-Jawarndima* (the lying one) because Lithi would often

Fig. 3.1 Senior Yanyuwa man Old Arthur Narnugawurruwurru, with *warnu* (chewing tobacco) at Doomadgee, in Queensland, northern Australia (Photograph: David Trigger c.1980). *Warnu* is the Yanyuwa language term for a ball of chewing tobacco that is mixed with the ash of bark from the Coolibah tree – *ma-warlan*. The ash itself is called *ma-mungkul*, and when added to the tobacco reduces its pH levels, thus increasing absorption, whilst also adding a distinctive taste. Martin and Trigger (2015: 284) note that in Garrwa the term for a ball of chewing tobacco is *Bundija*

say he would follow people into Borroloola but he would never come (Steve Johnston, in conversation with Bradley 1987).[2] Old Arthur's mother was a-Walwalmara, a Wurdaliya woman from Country to the south and south east of Vanderlin Island. His sister was Darby a-Muluwamara the mother of Annie a-Karrakayny.

Old Arthur went through his first initiation at a place called Liwurriya on the western side of the Wearyan River, to the far east of Borroloola, where the present day Manankurra pastoral station is located. He went through the higher-level initiation ceremonies of *a-Kunabibi* and *Kundawira* in the same area. During his youth he moved through the coastal area of the southwest Gulf of Carpentaria, traveling with family as they worked on pastoral properties across the region. It was during this time he met his wife Emily Peter, a Garrwa woman whose Country was the area around the mouth of the Calvert River.

Garrwa is a language group whose Country is located to the east of Yanyuwa Country. Old Arthur and Emily continued to move eastwards towards the Queensland border staying for a while on Wollogorang Station. They moved into Queensland and family oral tradition has it that Old Arthur was critical to helping establish Old Doomadgee (Dumaji) Mission at Bailey Point in 1933 and then the subsequent moving of this Mission in 1936 to its present location on the Nicholson River (Akehurst 2006). This mission run by the Open Brethren became home to large numbers of Garrwa, Waanyi and Ganggalida people and some Yanyuwa men, who like Old Arthur had married into Garrwa families. Domadgee is 400 kilometres southeast of Borroloola, in Queensland. Old Arthur was to spend the majority of the rest of his life at Doomadgee.[3] In Doomadgee he was known as Big Arthur.

Due to protection policies that were in place in the state of Queensland at that time, Old Arthur was unable to return to his home Country in the southwest Gulf of Carpentaria, and the township of Borroloola for over 50 years (see Trigger 1992).[4] It was only in 1980 that he came to return to Borroloola, travelling in the company of anthropologist David Trigger. He came to Borroloola to visit his family, including Annie a-Karrakayny, his classificatory brother Old Tim Rakawurlma and other family members, who he had not seen for many years. At this time, Annie mentioned to John Bradley (author), who lived in Borroloola and worked closely with families as a local school teacher, that Old Arthur was a man who held many important stories. In 1981 Old Arthur again travelled back to Borroloola from Doomadgee, this time accompanied by his nephew

Graham Friday Dimanyurru. Graham's mother Larrlya was a classificatory sister of Old Arthur. Travelling with Old Arthur at this time was his oldest son Keith Arthur Burrayi. Old Tim Rakawurlma had told Graham to bring Old Arthur across to Borroloola to be present for the *a-Kunabibi* ceremony which was to soon commence.[5] He was intended to stay for the entire ceremony which was approximately three and half months; however, Bradley was later informed by co-authors Dinah Norman a-Marrngawi and Annie a-Karrakayny, as well as senior Yanyuwa woman Eileen McDinny a-Manankurrmara that Old Arthur would not be able to stay for the duration of the full ceremony. He had thus given permission to a group of Rrumburriya clansmen, with close kinship bonds to Vanderlin Island, to perform the rituals on his behalf, and for his specific Country of North Island, Centre Island and Black and White Craggy Islands.

The Rrumburriya clan of Yanyuwa families comprise two distinct patrilineal groups. While these two patrilineal family groups consider themselves to be of the same Yanyuwa Rrumburriya clan overall, they are distinct from one another in that they hold ancestral ties to distinct areas of Rrumburriya territory within Yanyuwa Country. On the one hand, there is the 'island Rrumburriya' patrilineal group to which Old Arthur belonged associated with the island Country described as—North, Centre, Black Graggy and White Craggy Islands. On the other hand, there is the 'mainland/Vanderlin Island Rrumburriya' patrilineal group to which Old Tim Rakawurlma belonged, associated with Vanderlin Island and Rrumburriya Country in the vicinity of Borroloola. The island Rrumburriya group has ties to important sites associated with the White-bellied Sea Eagle Dreaming, while the mainland/Vanderlin Island Rrumburriya group has ties to important sites associated with the Tiger Shark Dreaming. However, both groups find a point of unity in their mutual association with the Dugong Hunter Dreaming Ancestors, whose journey crosses through all Rrumburriya island Country (see Bradley with Yanyuwa Families 2022). In addition, the Tiger Shark songline (*kujika*) that travels from Manankurra on the mainland northward to Walala (Lake Eames) on Vanderlin Island is also shared between these two distinct Rrumburriya patrilineal groups.

Over the years in the absence of the Arthur family from Borroloola, it was Old Tim Rakawurlma's family who had taken responsibility for the management of all Rrumburriya Country on the islands and all ceremony associated with it. However, in 1981 senior Yanyuwa men were insistent that Old Arthur and his sons return for ceremonial duties and perform the necessary rituals.

During this time at Borroloola (1980/1981) issues surrounding the partial success of the 1976 Yanyuwa land claim were still being discussed. Integral to many of these discussions was Annie a-Karrakayny, who had been left extremely disappointed by the legislative land claim process. She had been denied the opportunity to give evidence as a woman claimant, with only male claimants being invited to give testimonies to the court. Further, while the Rrumburriya Country of Vanderlin Island had been granted Aboriginal title by the Federal Land Commissioner Justice Toohey (1979), Annie's mother's Rrumburriya Country on North and Centre Islands had not been granted. People felt that their land had been split and broken apart by Justice Toohey's decision, and there was much discussion about how these things might be remedied. At the core of these discussions was the right of the island Rrumburriya group to be also able to speak for mainland Rrumburriya Country in the vicinity of Borroloola (see Fig. 3.2). There was emerging debate amongst Rrumburriya clan members and Rrumburriya people associated with Borroloola as to who had the right to claim this part of Country. The land claim process generally had bolstered the island Rrumburriya group's position at the expense of the mainland/Vanderlin Island Rrumburriya group, partly fuelled by the legislative process through which evidence is documented and decisions made, by lawyers, barristers, land councils and anthropologists, about who can talk for which parts of Country. The outcome also often reflects who has the whitefella political acumen to garner the greater attention of the lawyers, anthropologists and other 'experts' throughout this process. This contention set into play a political ruckus around Rrumburriya clan Country, and rights to assert ownership over the islands in the north of Yanyuwa Country (including North and Vanderlin Islands) and the mainland Rrumburriya Country at Borroloola.

For Annie, the return of her *kardirdi* Old Arthur to Borroloola had provided her with the opportunity to seek out knowledge about the Law for the Country for which she was *jungkayi* and from which she had been denied full restitution under the land claim. Deeply incensed by this situation she sought to 'straighten up' the Law by asking this old man to tell the story of succession as it related to mainland and island parts of Rrumburriya Country. Annie sought clarification on the events that had transpired to ensure that certain families, linked to particular lineages of Rrumuburriya clan Country, had come to be the rightful claimants to

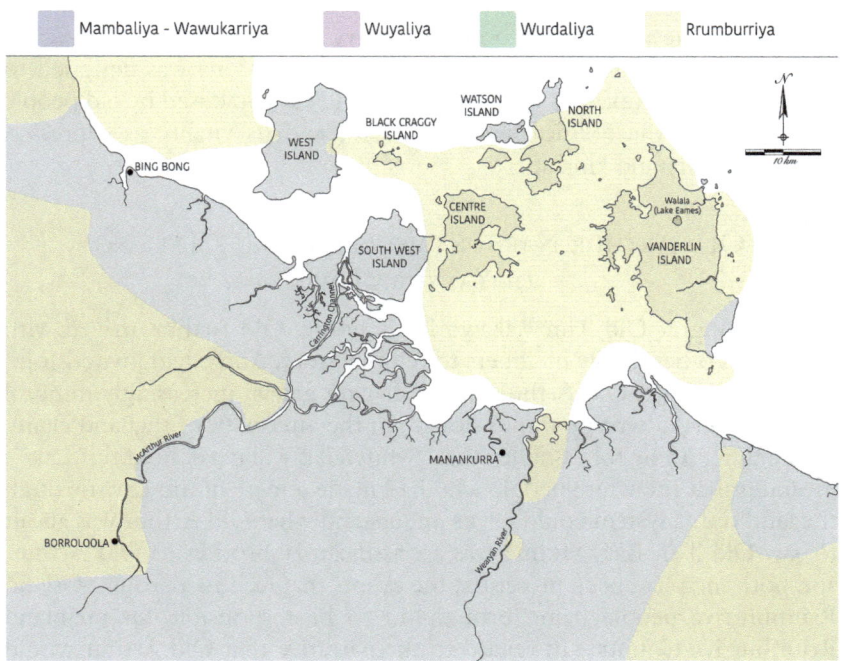

| | Mambaliya - Wawukarriya | | Wuyaliya | | Wurdaliya | | Rrumburriya |

Fig. 3.2 Map showing details of Rrumburriya clan Country

areas of island and mainland Country. More specifically she sought to learn the Law behind how island people had come to hold authority over mainland Rrumburriya parts of Country including Borroloola and parts of the McArthur River downstream. She knew the story in brief, but she and her mother's brother's son (*marruwarra*) Johnson Timothy and Whylo McKinnon wanted to know the details of how these events came to be. Further Old Tim Rakawurlma was not comfortable in telling this story without the presence of Old Arthur. This was in part due to whispers of gossip that certain island Rrumburriya people were taking over mainland Rrumburriya Country to which it was perceived they had no right, that they were "just putting themselves in" and thus "making a troubled Country". This rumour still prevails in Borroloola today and remains a catalyst for flair ups of tension in this community from time to time. Legislative land rights processes are known to have 'buggered up' (confused) the story for many parts of Yanyuwa Country (and are known to have had the same impact on the Country and Law of other Aboriginal claimant groups), and this exercise in iterating the Law was designed to straighten things up. This was how Law was always practised by old people and illustrates the political nature of Law, and its vitality as expressed through orality and kinship.

OLD ARTHUR NARNUNGAWURRUWURRU'S TELLING OF YANYUWA LAW

One evening at Old Tim Rakawurlma's home, Old Arthur arrived with Annie and other family members to tell this story. Annie had invited John Bradley to record Old Arthur's story, having grown increasingly mindful of the power of 'writing things down', in the aftermath of the land claim. At the time, Annie told Bradley that "whitefellas will never hold this Law", meaning that the white people who had made a mess of the Law through the land rights system could never understand what Old Arthur was about to say. Old Tim Rakawurlma was a classificatory brother to Old Arthur, and both men had been present at the events that lead to a group of island Rrumburriya people being brought in to be responsible for mainland Rrumburriya Country. In regard to the narrative that Old Arthur would share on this occasion, it is distinct in terms of the Yanyuwa language term given to this speech act. It was not described using the Yanyuwa verbs 'to talk' or 'to tell', rather the word *wirajkalmantharra* was used on this occasion. This is a very particular expression that is used when a specific kind of knowledge is to be transmitted. It is the kind of language used to describe instances when people would be given instruction in how a ceremony must be performed, or when talking about the path of songline. *Wirajkalmantharra* could be described as the verb that is used when matters of Law need to be told or narrated.

As Old Arthur told the story of how these relationships and bonds came to be, his words were affirmed by both Old Tim Rakawurlma and other senior men who had specific links to mainland Rrumburriya Country, Old Borroloola Willy Mundumundumara and Old Gordon Lansen Milyindirri.[6] Both of these men were classificatory brothers to Old Tim Rakawurlma and Old Arthur, and in attendance on the evening this story was recorded. At a later date, Annie described the actions of her *kardidi*, Old Arthur as "keeping the Law straight",

...he [Old Arthur] knew what was happening, everything was changing, but there still have to be boss for Country. That ceremony now (*Kundawira*) from the islands, made sure, there would also be boss. That ceremony now and that other one (*Kunumbu*) from this place Borroloola made sure everything was made straight, we have to remember that.

The two ceremonies mentioned here by Annie, the *Kundawira* and *Kunumbu*, are both high-level sacred ceremonies of the Rrumburriya clan. *Kundawira* is associated with the lineage of Rrrumburriya clan people that trace kinship to the White-bellied Sea Eagle Dreaming Ancestor and Dugong Hunter Dreaming Ancestors of the islands, and *Kunumbu* is associated with the mainland Rrumburriya clan people who share kinship with the Hill Kangaroo Dreaming Ancestor in the vicinity of the immediate Borroloola area.

The scope and reach of Old Arthur's narration on that evening was extensive and detailed, as perhaps it needed to be, for it was a long time since these matters had been discussed so publicly. It was also a demonstration of how actions firmly fixed in past actions of Law continued to be important in the present moment. Old Arthur's words convey a deeply held conviction of kincentric orientation; of ancestral Law, ceremonial potency, place empiricism and responsiveness to change. A thread that runs through the narrative is one which bonds the politics and authority of naming persons, naming of places in Country, and demarcating relationships between people and place as a mechanism by which individuals and groups are included and excluded.

Old Arthur reaches out to all manner of presences in the Yanyuwa lifeworld, to bring them into line with this thread of Law. This very act pulls together a tightly woven fabric of interacting elements. With his testimony became a legacy which continues to infuse political decision-making among Yanyuwa families, the granting of permissions and access to Country and the authority to speak about Country. In fact, the story of Old Arthur's testimony re-emerged as a point of community discussion in 2019, 2020 and 2021 due to the ongoing tension between some Rrumburriya families as to the rightful owners of island and mainland Country. These tensions reignite each time a senior Rrumburriya person passes away, and became revived in recent Facebook posts which triggered aggravation and disputes among some Rrumburriya people living in Borroloola. The need to assert and reiterate the Law through the telling of Old Arthur's narrative is made clear time and again in Borroloola. So let us now then turn to Old Arthur's narrative of Rrumburriya clan Country and learn how island people became bosses for mainland Country, through an artful interpretation of Law and political decision-making among senior Law holders.

We present each passage of this testimony in the original Yanyuwa text and then follow with its translation into English, as overseen by Mavis Timothy a-Muluwamara and John Bradley. We do this because Law holds its integrity through language and because the old people and Country only know Yanyuwa language. As Yanyuwa say, Country does not hear English.

Wabarrangu kiwa-ninya Burrulula malbu na-wini Jilbilyijibilyi kulu nyarrku barra na-wini Mundumundumara, Yanyuwamulu kulu nungka Binbingkamulu. Nya-mangaji malbu jibiya Burrulula, na-ngalki Rrumburriya. Jibiya Burrulula kulu bajarnu wayka Mirnngarra nankawa barra kulu wayka mili Jawuma baki Lhuka. Yiwa barra ka-arri wirdi ki-yarrambawajawu Kunumbu barra kurdukurdu nganjirra barni-ngantha barra nangurrbuwala nya-mangaji. Nya-mangaji wunala ka-wingka kariya nakari Mandungubu kulu kumba-yibanda Mabunji kulu kilu-wundarrba nankawa Burrulula, baji barra kilu-lhurruma Kunumbu, kilu-lhurruma kulu nyikungu yirriny kiwa-nbayaninya baji nya-mbangu wurnda ja-alarrinji baji nya-mbangu wirninymarr nyikungu yirriny nyuwu-mangaji ki-wunalawu.

A long time ago there was an old man at Borroloola and his name was Jilbilyijibilyi and he had another name Mundumundumara,[7] he spoke Yanyuwa and maybe he also spoke Binbingka,[8] he belonged to Borroloola. His clan was Rrumburriya. He belonged to Borroloola and also to Mirnngarra lagoon and down river to Jawuma (the Landing) and to Lhuka (Batten Point). He was the leader for the Kunumbu ceremony, it is secret and sacred and belongs to the Hill Kangaroo Dreaming. That Hill Kangaroo that came from the west from Mandungubu and he arrived at Mabunji [place name] and he named the lagoon at Borroloola and he danced the Kunumbu ceremony and his shredded feather body decoration fell to the ground the white barked gum tree around the lagoon are the shredded feathers.

Jilbilyijilbilyi kiwa-ninya alinda andaa a-nhanawaya a-Wuyaliya a-jibiya na-lukuluku na-manangka Wiliyurru nanda-wini a-Alanthaburra narnu-munanga. A-Kitty, anda barra a-ambirrijingu wukanyinjarra munanga wuka kandumba-yangama wuka yurrngumantha nya-alunga liyi-wajwajbalawu kanda-alarri rarra aluwa linji-wajbawajbalangku yanga-mantharra wuka kurda a-durijiwiji waraba rru-madamadawu biwali barra.

Jilbilyijilibilyi's wife was a Wuyaliya woman who came from the Crooked River, we call [that place] Wiliyurru. Her name was a-Alanthaburra, her English name was Saltwater Kitty, she was the first woman to speak English. She would stand amongst the white people and she would translate words from English to Yanyuwa and from Yanyuwa to English. The poor thing she would stand there in a dress, not a possum fur apron.

Wula barra kawula-wingka waykaliya waliyangu barra linji-malarngula, kawula-wingka ambirri ki-yarrambawajawu, walyangku barra nguthunda-kari waliyangu kulu arnindawangu yurrngumantha.

Those two [Jilbilyijibilyi and Saltwater Kitty] they would go down to the sea to hunt dugong with all the family. They would travel for ceremony and then again dugong, they were always on the coast and the islands.

Bawuji wabarrangu li-jakarda kala-ninya akarru Yulbarra. Awunga nga-malakarimba, nungka yarrambawaja ka-arri baji li-jakarda kala-ninya baji li-malbumalbu li-bardibardi li-yumbuwarra marda. A-kurdukurdu a-muwarda Rrumburriya nya-mangaji awara, wula barra kawula-ninya baji barra. Mili nyarrku wuka jirna-nanji kujika ja-walanymanji Yulbarra ja-wingkayi kariya nakari Manankurra ja-wundirrinji barra kujika ki-adumungku barra.

So, it was a long time ago and there were many people there at Yulbarra (on the south-central west coast of Vanderlin Island). There was a ceremony there, there were old people and young people and many canoes. That Country is Rrumburriya and those two were there [Jilbilyijibilyi and Saltwater Kitty]. There is just another small story I will tell you at this point, the songline [kujika] is coming out of the sea at Yulbarra it has been coming from the southwest from Manankurra and it is climbing out of the sea at Yulbarra, it is the songline for the Tiger Shark.

Kawula-arri baji Yulbarra nya-mangaji malbu Jilbilyijilbilyi kulu yikurra-wangu a-Alanthaburra. Kawula-arri kawula-ninya barra, kulu yiwa almir-rmantharra almirr ka-arri yilaa yiwa kilu-almirrngantha ardu, buyi ardu ka-arri wulumantharra nyungkarrku ki-awaralu baji barra ngunthunda-kari waliyangu kila-ka lama kurdardi barra lama bujayi janyka bujayi wankala wuka kila-ka barra yuwu bujayi ki-wanakalawu na-jumanykarrawarda nya-mangaji ardu buyi wungkuwungkuwarda barra kalngi. Jina barra ardu ardirri kumbu-ngka baji Yulbarra ka-wajba ki-malbungku ngaliwa ka-arri baji almirr. "Biyi! Biyi! Bawuji jirna-wakaramanji karna-yanjarrila nakari jina awara anthawirriyarra barra". Bawuji wungkuwungkulamba malbu ka-lhuwarri ka-arri mirdan ki-ardungku, ka-arri anku "Ngabiyarra ardirri ka-wingka ngathangkalu wun-

dururra, baku barra nya-ngalinga ardu ka-yanjarrila". Bawuji a-mangaji
a- Kitty kanda-arri a-walkurru, kulu malbu kalilu-yalbanga alunga li-jibiya
nguthundakari li-malbumalbu barranamba li-ngatha wunyatha Vanderlin
Island Jack, Rrakawurlma na-wini nyiki-biyi ki-Old Tim wunhaka ngatha,
Banjo kulu Old Leo Yulungurri jibiya Manankurra nya-mangaji, nyarrku
barra malbu Jack Baju nyiki-biyi ki-Musso mili nyarrku Jack Buyinymanda
bawuji kalinymaba-wukalwukanyinjaninya yurrngumantha yiku ki-
ardirriyu. Baku barra baku nya-mangaji ardu ka-yanjarri nyiki-ardu ki-
malbungku, mili yurrulu Jilbilyijilbilyi kulu li-mangaji li-wirdi
nyuwu-mangaji ki-awarawu nguthundakari kalinyamba-
wukalwukanyinjaninya kulu wakara kalilu-lhaa nya-mangaji ardu
bardarda barra jibiya nguthundakari yiwa barra ka-arri nyiki-wayarungu
barra kumbu-ngka baji Yulbarra yiwa barra ka-arri wurranganji aluwa li-
wirdiwalangu li-anthawirriyarra. Li-mangaji li-malbumalbu kalilu-
ngunda na-wini na-wunyingu barra kalilu-wundarrba Lhawulhawu
ki-adumungku barra baku barra li-wajbala kalilu-ngunda Pharaoh kalu-
wundarrba nganinya.

So those two were there at Yulbarra, that old man Jilbilyijilbilyi and his
wife a-Alanthaburra. They were there and that old man [Jilbilyijilbilyi] had
a dream and in the dream, he saw a young boy with long black hair and he
was running with a stone axe and he called out, "Daddy! Daddy! I have
found you and I will be born from this Country, from this saltwater
Country!" So early in the morning that old man knew a child was to be born
and he said to his wife, "A spirit child came to me last night and a child will
be born for us".[9] Saltwater Kitty was there and she was pregnant and the old
man went and spoke to the old men who were the owners of the Country,
Vanderlin Island Jack, the father for Old Tim, Banjo and Leo who came
from Manankurra and Jack Baju father for old Musso and Jack Buyinymanda.
So, they talked and talked about that spirit child. Later, much later that child
was born, it was a son for that old man Jilbilyijilbilyi and then all of the
senior men for Vanderlin Island knew then that the child had come from
their Country, that he belonged to the water of that Country, from Yulbarra.
He was a child belonging to the saltwater people. The old men they gave
that baby boy a bush name Lhawulhawu, it belongs to the Tiger Shark
Dreaming, in English he was known as Pharaoh.

Nya-mangaji malbu Pharaoh ka-yirdardi Rrumburriya anthawirriyarra
mili nyarrku barra wuka yurrulu ka-arri mayangku marda kangka
nyiki-murimuri jibiya Burrulula nangurrbuwala barra, nya-mangaji malbu
Lhawulhawu jibiya Burrulula baki jibiya nguthundakari waliyangu kany-
marda awara. Awara nyiyiki-murimuriyu Burrulula, wayka wulanginda
Jawuma, Lhuka barra kulu nya-mangaji nankawa Mirnngarra, a-Marndiwa

rriku kanda-arri akarru Liwurriya, Manankurra akarramba li-malbumalbu
jalu-yinbayi kanymarda kujika nyikungu nya-mangaji jibiya Manankurra
nya-alunga liyi-Rrumburriyawu ki-waliyanguyu kulu nya-mangaji ki-
mardumbarrawu jibiya Yalku kariya nyala waykaliya ja-wingkayi ngaliba
Nguwangkila.

That old man Pharoah he grew up on the islands. He was a saltwater man
but he also belonged to the mainland because his father's father was from
Borroloola and a Hill Kangaroo Dreaming man. So that old man Pharoah
Lhawulhawu he also belonged to Borroloola, but he also belonged to the
island Country to the north. The Country for his father's father was
Borroloola downstream to Jawuma and Lhuka and Mirnngarra. The
Marndiwa initiation ceremony for that old man [as a young boy] was held
at Liwurriya, Manankurra is on the east bank of the Wearyan River, and
Liwurriya on the west. The old men sang two songlines for him, they sang
the *kujika* for the islands, the Tiger Shark and the *kujika* from the mainland,
the Saltwater Crocodile Dreaming that comes from Yalku Gorge downstream all the way to Nguwangkila (on the Batten Creek).

Wurrbi barra nya-mangaji malbu kiwa-ninya wirriyarra nguthundakari
barra ki-yarrambawajala ki-kujikala kilu-manha barra nya-mangaji
malbu ka-arri mulungka yilaa ki-anthawu ki-ankawangu.

Now truly through the Law that old man [Lhawulhawu – Pharoah]
belonged to the islands and held the ceremonies. The kujika also sat on his
tongue for the islands and mainland.

Ka-arri wanjilirra bajingulaji Wulkuwulku, bajingu li-malbumalbu li-
Rrumburriya li-jibiya nguthundakari kalu-arri, "Barra bawuji kanilu-
rdumala jina mirningiya kulu kanilu-ngundala yiku barruwa
ki-Kundawirawu nya-nganunga yarrambawaja warriya arrkula mirningiya
kiwa-ninya alanjila wunumbarra mungku-alakalangka kiwa-ninya kulu
ka-wajba akarru "kuyu wurrwilhi kuyu wurrwilhi wayi jamarndarrka" kulu
nalarrku barra li-mirningu kalu-lharnangantha karakarra nakari ambirri
"waraba waraba" kurda yurrngumanthalulu warriya. Barra bawuji kanilu-
ngunda yiku ki-malbungku yumbulyumbulmantha, kurdukurdu nya-
mangaji nganjirra barra, wurrbi barra anthawirriyarrawu ngayamantharra
liyi-mirningu waraba barra nalarrku liyi-rdurduwarrawu kalu-yinba
kujika wundarurra kalu-lhurrama ngabungabula nya-mangaji
yarrambawaja nya-alunga liyi-maramaranjawu kulu rruwu-mangaji rru-
karnkarnkawu rraja-murimuri rra-ngatha ngarna wirriyarra.

The old man [Lhawulhawu – Pharoah] was an a-Kunabibi [ceremony]
initiate at Wulkuwulku, that place on Kangaroo Island, and then from there
the old Rrumburriya men from the islands said, "Alright we will give him
the ceremony marks from our Kundawira ceremony, that is our ceremony

the poor thing, it is that ceremony that began when one old man would sit in a platform in the camp and called out, 'Hey! Hey! White-bellied Sea Eagle do you have any white shredded feather body decoration?' And those other men on the ceremony ground would call out", No! No! All the way like that, all day they would call out. It is only for proper men that ceremony, it is totally restricted, it is not for newly initiated young men. They would sing kujika [songlines] at night and dance in the late afternoon, it was the ceremony for the Dugong Hunter Dreaming and the White-bellied Sea eagle. She is my most senior paternal grandmother, she is my spiritual essence, I am her spiritual heir.

Ngalalu li-welfare ka-wingka marnajinju kalalu-jukujukuma li-jakarda li-wulu, li-bardibardi, li-ardibirri marda li-jakarda li-anthawirriyarra. Kalalu-jukujukuma kari-nguthunda, karakarra, kari-wayka barra kulu kalalu-darlbirrantha Burrulula warriya! Li-mangaji li-malbumalbu li-jibiya waliyangu kala-ninya Burrulula akarrimba baku barra Malarndarri akarrikarimba. Nya-mangaji malbu Jilbilyijilbilyi ka-malburri malbu kiwaninya kurdandu kanilu-ngunda nyiki-ardu Kunumbu ka-arri yiku bawuji kumba-mirrala yinda wirdi barra kirna-ngunda barra yinku walakurrawala kurdukurdu barra.

When welfare came to this place[10] [southwest Gulf of Carpentaria] they rounded everyone up, many men, old women, middle aged people and children and all of the saltwater people. They rounded them up from the north, from the east and from downstream and they dumped them all at Borroloola, the poor things! The old men from the islands now lived at Borroloola, some sat on the west bank at Borroloola while others lived on the east bank at Malarndarri. That old man Jilbilyijilbilyi he was really old and he had given his son the Kunumbu ceremony from that Country before he died, he told him he was also boss for the Borroloola Country and he gave to him all the Law for that Country.

Bawuji ngala wula malbu wujara Old Tim kulu Banjo malbu kawulamba-kajakajama li-ardubirri kalu-yanjarri Burrulula nya-mangaji malbu jibiya Burrulula Jilbilyijilbilyi kulu nyiki-ardu Pharaoh barra kawula-arri wulanga, "Marnalu li-mangaji liyiwulanga-ardubirri li-jibiya marnajingulaji Burrulula jalini likili-wayurungu barra bawuji kanawula-ngunda yimbalanga Kunumbu kulu bawuji yirru li-jibiya nguthundakari kulu nganu li-jibiya marnaji mayangka kanu-wunumbarrirrijala kulu kananmala arrkula barra bawuji bajingu jalini arrkula likili-nganji barra kiyarrambawajala marda ardirri kangka".

So when Old Tim and Old Banjo had children and they were born at Borroloola that old man who belonged to Borroloola – Jilibilyijilbilyi, and his son Pharoah they said to them, "Here they are, your children, they belong to this Country Borroloola, their spirits have bathed in the water of this Country, we will give to you the Kunumbu ceremony [for mainland Rrumburriya] and you people from the north [island Rrumburriya] and we people from this Country will be kinsmen, we will be as one for the ceremonies of this Country, this is because of the actions of the spirit children".

Bawuji barra ngalalu li-ardubirri nya-alunga li-mangaji li-jibiya nguthundakari kalu-yanjarri baji Burrulula li-wirdiwalangu li-jibiya Burrulula kalalu-ngunda na-wini na-wunyingu barra nya-mangaji kajakaja Johnson kalu-wundarrba Ngayijbungayijbulama nangurrbuwala nya-mangaji na-wini nakari waliyangu nyiki-biyi kilu-nganda Babarramila liyi-maramaranjawu kulu nyarrku na-wini ngaliwa ardu Mananjana, warriyangalayawu ki-kujikala nya-mangaji.

When the children belonging to the men from the islands were born at Borroloola, they also belonged to Borroloola and they were given names from that Country, just like my classificatory son here Johnson – Ngayibungayijbulama is his name, that is from the Hill Kangaroo Dreaming. But his name from the islands was Babarramila, for the Dugong Hunter Dreaming. And he has another name from the islands Mananjana that is for the Hammerhead Shark, that is a kujika name.

Jina barra wankala wuka narnu-yuwa barra narnu-Yanyuwa na-yuwa ki-awarawu yarrambawajawu yarrambawaja baki ardirri wunungu barra barranamba ngabiya ngabiya barra politics ki-wajbalawu narnu-munanga narnu-yuwa na-nganunga politics wurra ki-awarala jiwini ki-kujikala ki-yarrambawajala wurrbi bajuwarnu barra na-yuwa ki-awarawu jiwini yulurr.

This is a story from the old days, it is a story of Law. Yanyuwa Law for the Country and ceremonies, the ceremony and spirit children are strong. It is like...what would you call it? Yes, it is like politics for the white people, it is like the law for white people, well this is our politics and it lives deep in the Country, in the kujika, in the ceremonies. Truly this is the Law for the Country for all time.

Old Arthur's narrative makes no concessions for western conceptions of law; rather, the nature of the subject matter is constructed for a Yanyuwa audience, and many subjects are referred to in terms that sound, at least to western ears, vague. This is because people in small, culturally homogenous communities often have much shared knowledge and do not need to be continually explicit about such things. It is assumed that the listeners will be able to infer what the speaker is talking about. When matters such as spirit child conception, ceremony or *kujika* are being discussed and, by extension, subjects of a sacred nature, then people often use cryptic or indirect expressions to convey knowledge. This was the case with Old Arthur's testimony. The challenge, then, in this recollection of Law is how to decode this narrative for the benefit of an interested readership without compromising the delicate nature of this knowledge embedded as it is in the land, sea and kinship that contextualises its sharing. It would be easy to read this text and overlook the potency of political rhetoric that it contains due to an untranslatability which separates western and Indigenous, specifically Yanyuwa, understandings.

Kinship operates as the primary organising principle throughout Old Arthur's testimony, but the kind of kinship he details goes well beyond human-to-human relations. It has relational scope to link all living and non-living presences in Country and to specifically orient people through relations with spiritual beings, Dreaming ancestors and places (Bradley with Yanyuwa Families 2022; Kearney 2021). Names are very important, as seen in the act of giving Pharoah the bush name of Lhawulhawu. He is a mainland person and he is given a name from the islands; he is both a Hill Kangaroo Dreaming person as well as a Tiger Shark Dreaming person. Pharoah's bush name Lhawulhawu ties him to the saltwater Country of Vanderlin Island from which his *ardirri* (spirit child) originated. This name, drawn from the Tiger Shark Dreaming, illustrates an inseparable link between him and that place Yulbarra on Vanderlin Island that has substantial ramifications for his right to hold and wield the ceremony and Law for that Country. A similar practice of giving two names also happened with Yanyuwa elder Johnson Timothy. Johnson was the father of Philip Timothy Narnungawurruwurru, the young man who gave the next iteration of this Law in 2000, to which we will soon turn our attention. Johnson's spirit child came from Borroloola so he was given the bush name Ngayijbungayibulama (a name associated with the Hill Kangaroo Dreaming place at the river crossing in Borroloola), but he also had a bush name for the islands, Babarramila, which is a name relating to the Dugong Hunter Dreaming. These names speak to the reality and bonds between mainland and island Rrumburriya people, born of these specific moments in the continuation of Yanyuwa Law.

Yanyuwa have navigated and sustained the continuity of their Law over lifetimes in which change has occurred. At times this change has been recognised and accommodated through political decision-making, and a reaching of consensus amongst elders, as illustrated by Old Arthur's recollections of Law in action. In other times Yanyuwa have had to work incredibly hard to make sense of the external intrusions into their cultural life which have prompted reformulations of their world and the praxis of Law within it. Few have been so significant as the demands brought about by legislative land rights.

The making and unmaking of Aboriginal land claimants has a complex history reflected in the evolution of statutory declarations, and legislative instruments themselves. These complexities are also evident in the juridical interpretations and applications of British common law, the scrutinising of evidence, the receipt of Indigenous testimonies and the subjecting of Aboriginal claimants to cross-examination on their identity and existence. Presented with this as the only pathway to assert their right to Country, an act that is required and in accordance with their Law and standing as *ngimirringki* and *jungkayi*, Yanyuwa have both urgently and patiently sought restitution on these western legal terms, but it has been hard and at times heart breaking. Annie's experience of having rights to her Country denied in the first legislative land claim and only partially returned through a subsequent retrial demonstrates this elongated hardship. The specific design of legislative land rights, the mobilising of legal definitions of aboriginality, traditional ownership, ongoing connection and the evidentiary demands placed upon Aboriginal people are what turn Law people into 'claimants' (see Kearney 2022). These are processes that construct and hold in place fundamental social classifications through which individuals are known by officials, and potentially, over the long term, themselves. As Adgemis (2017: 209) writes,

> ...there is a growing separation between those who have the capacity and knowledge to navigate and negotiate legal and technical forums for land management and those who are knowledgeable about Law. This situation is an enabler for those who do not necessarily know the relevant Law or have the right to speak for places in question to become influential beyond what was previously possible.

These become the conditions which determine how people are allowed to act and potentially how they choose to act and they are also the conditions in which Yanyuwa must find ways and means to hold strong in their Law. The motivation to continue to try is strong, and this next part of this story of Yanyuwa Law must be read for its expression of Law as realpolitik.

Yanyuwa Law and Legislative Land Rights

The Royal Commission into Aboriginal land rights in the Northern Territory conducted by Justice Albert Edward Woodward between 1973 and 1974 lay the foundation for Australia's first legislative land rights redress scheme, the *Aboriginal Land Rights (Northern Territory) Act 1976* (ALRA) (Australian Government 1976). The ALRA has provided Aboriginal people with an avenue to seek restitution of lands and some waters, in the form of freehold title, based on legal determinations of traditional ownership and enduring connections to Country. Under the ALRA claimants are required to present evidence to a Commonwealth-appointed judge (a Land Commissioner), supported by anthropologists, lawyers and other 'experts'. The Land Commissioner then makes a final recommendation on the validity of this evidence for traditional ownership.

Yanyuwa launched the first claim ever to be heard under the ALRA (Avery and McLaughlin 1977; Bradley 1992, 2000; Seton and Bradley 2005; Kearney 2018), and did so for several reasons; firstly, because they are resolutely *li-Anthawirriyarra*—that is saltwater people whose ancestors come from this Country (Bradley 2008); secondly, because they had no choice but to pursue this legal avenue for any restorative justice; and thirdly, because they had been denied their ancestral right to their Country through processes of colonial theft. Describing the land claim experience, Billy Miller Rijirrngu (2002, in Kearney 2018: 195) recalls:

> I was feeling you know that I was fighting for the land that should be mine… I was getting more and more involved in the fight for Country where I come from and I tell him the Land Commissioner about my grandfather's country and my Country… We got long list of brothers, two fathers we had, and all the young fella coming up behind too, they got Country too…you know most of those people who were at the meeting [land claim] have all gone, there's only a few of us left…most of the people have died and it's a sad thing for me to see cause they been there and fought for it and then you know its taken so long to be handed back.

The decision to claim lands and waters under the ALRA was made collectively by Yanyuwa women and men in 1976. This was the beginning of what remains one of the longest running Indigenous land rights cases in Australian history (Kearney 2018, 2022). The 1976 land claim resulted in only a partial granting of claimed land to the Yanyuwa claimants. Women were largely excluded from the claim process, reflecting the bias of a western legal system. In 1992, a subsequent land claim was lodged for the lands not recognised as Yanyuwa lands in the 1976 claim. This claim was met with substantial delay and resistance from the Northern Territory government and other private white interests, and was only finalised in 2015 (see Young 2009; Kearney 2018 for detailed explanation of the reasons for such a substantial delay). In 2000 Yanyuwa embarked on one of "the most radical moves to restitute sea Country in recent Australian settler colonial history" (Kearney 2018: 195). They sought title to over 120 km of intertidal sea Country. While the Land Commissioner determined that Aboriginal title ought to be vested in the claimants, the land claimed was never granted. This can occur because, although the Land Commissioner can find that Aboriginal title ought to be granted to claimants, ultimate discretion lies with the Northern Territory Minister to sign off on such grants and approve the vestige of freehold Aboriginal title as recommended.

Aboriginal people frequently find participating in the processes of land claim evidence and testimony difficult, infuriating and upsetting. Claimants are often invited or asked to give evidence in regard to their community's Law or ceremonies in ways that demand they explain something over which they have no right to speak. Deborah Rose (1995, 1996, 2000) writes of these issues with great clarity. For example, Rose (1996: 38–39, 2000: 114) describes the difficultly faced by women claimants in the Jasper Gorge/Kidman Springs land claim,[11] where they ultimately decided that they could not share a secret/sacred women's ceremony with the male Land Commissioner and overwhelmingly male legal staff. A senior woman explained, "From Dreaming right up till now no man been look that thing. We can't lose that Law", carrying with it the consequence of women being unable to combat the anthropological and western legal presumptions of patrilineal control and knowledge of their own lands.

Aboriginal claimants are often made to draw boundaries between one another and in doing so sow social division within communities through the land claim process. For Yanyuwa many of these acts also feel like a breach of Law, as they do not follow rules of succession, and proper kincentric lines for knowing and speaking about Country and Law. Rose (2000: 87) also points to an analogous example of senior Yarralin woman Dora Jilpngarri,[12] who vigorously rejected answering questions about patrilineal sub-categories of Yarralin identity, and who declined to participate in land claim proceedings for the same reason. From this Rose (2000: 87) concludes that:

[l]and claims required that at some level people sort themselves into those who will act as claimants, will assert primary responsibility for the country, and will, if successful, receive title to land. The process of sorting necessarily means that some people will be excluded.

Further discussion of gender bias and discrimination against women in the *Aboriginal Land Rights (Northern Territory) Act 1976* legislation and process is provided by Toussaint et al. (2001: 163–164), who make a case for the need for female Land Commissioners, of which there has never been one. There has never been an Indigenous Land Commissioner either.

PHILLIP TIMOTHY NARNUNGAWURRUWURRU'S STORY: SPEAKING ABOUT LAW IN 2000

The next time the details of Rrumburriya clan ownership across the islands and mainland stretches of Yanyuwa Country would become a point of public discussion and debate was during the 2000 Yanyuwa sea grass beds and riverbanks land claim. This claim, again under the ALRA, is referred to as the *Lhungkannguwarra—People of the Mangroves: Sea Country Claim* (2000). It brought together a collective of multi-generational Yanyuwa claimants (Bradley 2000; Kearney 2018: 195–196; Seton and Bradley 2005: 37–38). The elders among the claimants were well versed in the production that is an on-Country land claim hearing,[13] having been part of the previous ALRA claim in 1992, while others were stepping into adult claimant roles for the first time in their lives. Mid-generation Yanyuwa, and those aged in their early 30s, were encouraged to stand up before the Land Commissioner and give evidence for the first time, of their traditional ownership and genealogy as woven into Country and through clan membership. The 2000 sea Country claim is ongoing due to governmental reluctance on behalf of both the Northern Territory and Federal Governments to accept the findings of the Land Commissioner. These legislative efforts chart a period in Australian social and legal history, revealing the uncomfortable tension at the basis of two laws that operate in this part of Australia.

Philip Timothy, aged in his early 30s at the time, was listed on the claim as a senior Rrumburriya clan member and was called upon to give testimonial evidence regarding who held responsibility over a certain area of intertidal sea Country in the Gulf. He was also instructed by Annie a-Karrakayny and his senior father's brother Whylo McKinnon to explain how it was that he was an island Rrumburriya man who could speak for mainland Rrumburriya Country. To support him in this process was Annie a-Karrakayny who raised the point of the historical processes as described by Old Arthur in 1981. By 2000, many senior men had died, including Philip's father Johnson Timothy. Philip's classificatory father's brother Old Whylo McKinnon was present at the hearing, but very ill. Philip carried the same bush name as Old Arthur, Narnungawurruwurru. In Yanyuwa kinship terms, Annie called Philip her *kardirdi*, her classificatory mother's brother (uncle), which is the same kinship term she used for Old Arthur. In the context of the bush camp set up for the duration of the land claim hearing on-Country, Annie spoke to Philip and told him the story of how the union between the mainland and island Rrumburriya groups had taken place. She explained to him that it was he, in the absence of the old men, who must now tell the story to the Land Commissioner so as to be sure to straighten up the Law.

John Bradley was in attendance as the consulting anthropologist on the land claim for Yanyuwa families. While Philip was identified by senior Yanyuwa men and women as the right person to speak for that Country, Bradley recalls that Philip was daunted by the prospect of having to explain, in English for a western legal audience, a complex transfer of authority and responsibility for Country from one Rrumburriya lineage to another. In the lead up to having to give this evidence in the land claim, Philip expressed his doubts to Bradley about his capacity to relay this depth of Law in front of the Land Commissioner and his Yanyuwa kin, remarking "How am I going to do this?". Nonetheless, with the support and assistance of Annie and fellow Yanyuwa elders Billy Miller Rijirrngu, Whylo McKinnon and Steve Johnston Jnr, Philip recounted a version of Old Arthur's story in front of the judge, lawyers, anthropologists and a large group of Yanyuwa families.

Justice Olney, the Land Commissioner at the time, asked directly how it was that the island Rrumburriya group to which Philip belonged were able to speak for and give evidence on mainland Rrumburriya Country. Philip had listened intently to the elders, and they had talked him through what Old Arthur had explained in 1981. What is ultimately recorded in the transcript from the land claim hearing is a very cursory version of what happened. The details of what was spoken of behind the scenes was not etched into the legal record—land claim evidence rarely engages with the depth of intellectual insight that defines Indigenous Law. Evidence is often quite laconic and is forensic only in regard to matters upon which a well-developed and extensive body of literature exists, which itself speaks to the intersection of ethnography, anthropology and legal practice (Sutton 2003; Burke 2011; Trigger 2004; Trigger et al. 2013; Glaskin 2017). The formal court process requires that Aboriginal people be scrutinised, questioned and examined in English, by a judge and legal councils, in regard to their own Law. This places the onus upon Aboriginal people to respond in sufficient detail, sophistication and translational clarity in order to assert the place and knowledge of their own Law, while simultaneously accounting for the lack of cultural and linguistic knowledge held by the non-Indigenous people involved in these legal processes (Cooke 1995; Walsh 2008, 2011; Nash and Henderson 2002).

The transcript from Phillip's evidence to the judge, given via questioning by council assisting the Yanyuwa claimants, gives little indication of the pressure that Phillip was under and what was being demanded of him in the context of a very public hearing. Nor does it give any indication of the background support that he was being given by his elders who were speaking to him in language and affirming what he was saying. There is an additional evidentiary burden here; Philip is being asked to speak to ritual and ceremonial matters that he himself had never been initiated into and yet this evidence was central to progressing a truthful account of the legislative land claim. Phillip had been through *a-Kunabibi* but not *Kundawira* and was thus having to articulate Law which he was not initiated into himself.

What follows here is a transcript from the proceedings of the Lhukannguwarra land claim from 21 June 2000 relating to Philip's right as an island Rrumburriya clansperson to speak for mainland Rrumburriya Country in accordance with the Law that Old Arthur had explained 19 years earlier in 1981. Note that Mr Parsons is the barrister representing the Yanyuwa families:

| Mr Parsons: | All right then. Now Philip Timothy, you have got that thing [microphone] – I might as well speak on – Philip, now, David (*Rrumburriya man, David Roper a claimant to Borroloola Country down to the Batten Point through his father, Borroloola Willy*) we have got as *ngimirringki* and he is the last one, the last- and brother- he has got a brother there- for ceremony, what does that mean if there's only that many *ngimirringkis* as |

	young as he is? Can he do the- can he perform the role himself for that Country?
Philip Timothy:	Yeah. Well, you see, before – long time ago, maybe before dad was alive, when grandfather, they used to carry this under Law which was on top of that *Kunabibi*,[14] it was real sacred, and not many people talk about it you know. Before we used to be separated, like that island Rrumburriya mob, out on the island, and we'd left all the mainland Rrumburriya there. We all used to be separated first before, a long time ago.
Mr. Parsons:	Right
Philip Timothy:	Yeah, because that eagle (White-Bellied Sea Eagle [Dreaming Ancestor] – which I can't call the name because I'm not *Jungkayi*, I might get Billy (*Billy Miller is jungkayi*) to call the name of the bird.
Billy Miller:	*a-Karnkarnka*
Mr. Parsons:	*a-Karnkarnka*
Dr. Bradley:	*a-Karnkarnka*. White-bellied Sea Eagle
Philip Timothy:	And kangaroo. They had separate business, real strong sacred business. The kangaroo had his and that bird has his. Then later on all the tribes, all the mainland Rrumburriya mob and island Rrumburriya mob, got together and shared the same business because the kangaroo was Rrumburriya too, and that bird. Rrumburriya, but they'd been separated before but they got – everybody got together now and we all share the same ceremony today.
Mr. Parsons:	Right. Who told you that?
Philip Timothy:	Well, by my father, Billy and my grandfather
Mr. Parsons:	That's *kangku* for you, your father's father
Philip Timothy:	Yeah
Mr. Parsons:	Right, all right. So what is – can you explain to the judge how it is – is that the reason why you – the island Rrumburriya come into this Country for mainland and share?
Philip Timothy:	Yep
Mr. Parsons:	Is there any other reason that you mob come in or is it through that....?
Philip Timothy:	Well it's through that now.

Mr. Parsons: Right
Philip Timothy: Through that ceremony.

The details that Philip managed to convey were rather oblique, which of course is the norm when talking about matters of real sensitivity. Even though brief, Philip's telling of the events spoke to a demand for the expression of relationality in regard to Country and kin. Tragically Philip would pass away in 2007, rendering memory of his testimony and participation in the 2000 land claim with a potent sense of loss for his future as a Law man in this community. It also brings pride for his family and members of the Rrumburriya clan. The retelling of both men's testimonies is central to the workings of oral traditions; where knowledge and insights are emplaced from the moment a person begins to speak. Philip's telling is therefore laconic, as it needed to be. There was much that could not be said, but in the way of oral traditions in small-scale communities, all of the Yanyuwa listeners of his testimony understood what was going on.

Even as recent as February 2021 Graham Friday Dimanyurru asked for a further retelling and reading of all the events described above, and other people have requested to hear both Philip's and Old Arthur's stories retold, embracing the fact that this Law was written down, thus now cannot be easily disputed, and can also be mobilised through retelling as time and circumstances demand. Yet, the very process of 'writing down' the Law changes the story; an event that was embedded in deep orality and particular praxis as demonstrated by Old Arthur is transformed. Through the land claim process and the demand of transcripts for legal analysis, and even Annie Karrakayny's demand for the recording and transcription of Old Arthur's testimony, all lead to the representation of Law in forms and mediums which betray its substance. Old Arthur's telling of the events and Philips's retelling of these same events still however demonstrate that individuals and communities privilege knowledge according to their own criteria, taste, proclivities and, importantly, contemporary needs.

Both texts are highly political as to the nature of assertions to Country. Disputes over the right to speak for Country remain such that disputes continue to emerge around who is a proper Rrumburriya saltwater person and a proper Rrumburriya mainland person despite the circulation of knowledge attached to these testimonies. It would seem that the matter of contest never rests in this close and kincentrically bound community, and this is the realpolitik of identity and belonging as bound to Law. There is a persistent sense of urgency in this community to write things down, and most importantly to write them down properly, in language and in translation to mitigate against confusion and misrepresentations that might take hold among those who do not fully know the Law or do not remember Old Arthur's and later Philip's iterations of this Law.

A Word on Pushing Orality into Written Forms

The story we share here demonstrates the falsity of the often-held misconception that there is always a literal translation of words in Indigenous languages such as Yanyuwa in English; a misguided assumption that different cultural perspectives are bridgeable by related concepts in English, word-for-word (Bradley with Yanyuwa Families 2022). As Niranjana (1998: 134) explains, colonised peoples are faced with the subtle yet devastating necessity of translating their political frameworks into the languages of their colonisers,

> ...language of what we may call capital and community, where we experience a permanent lack of fit, given these languages never mesh together smoothly...There are different – often mutually unintelligible – languages of the political (as also languages in the ordinary sense of the word) which inhabit our space and configure our questions and interests.

Vazquez (2011: 27–28) frames language as delineating the borders of "a given system of meaning and more generally, of a given epistemic territory", and the translation of non-western language, and therefore knowledge, into Eurocentric languages is modernity's enforcement of western metaphysical principles and thus enforcement of western parameters of legibility and mutual recognition.

> The demise of oral traditions and the institution of a scriptural economy of knowledge comes hand in hand with the erasure of the past... The notions of memory (ancestors/memoria), land (tierra) and language (palabra) represent examples of the untranslatable, namely that which is erased by translation and replaced by the modern notions of chronology, space and writing... Coloniality has performed this uprooting of the "non-western", this un-naming, in order to inscribe them in a system of classification as the other, the backward, the savage, the primitive other. Translation is here revealed as erasure.

THE PRACTICE OF LAW

This chapter has told a story of Yanyuwa Law by sharing the testimonies of two Yanyuwa men, born decades apart, but who carried the same name and belonged to the same clan Country. These testimonies were given in vastly different contexts and situations, in the first instance, in the company of a small group of family and close kin, and in the second, although still in the company of family, to a white audience of legal and other 'experts'. The two situations are made distinct by the particularities of audience, language, generational expressions of knowledge, colonial pressures, lifestyle changes and the positionality of each speaker, yet the content of both testimonies, in many respects, follows the same rules of conduct and expression. These are rules which have always underpinned Yanyuwa Law. The first is a kincentric orientation. The second is that there remains an empiricism in Country that comes from *ngalki*, an essence which cannot be extinguished. The third is that both testimonies express fundamental rules as to the realpolitik that is expressed in Yanyuwa orality, collective decision-making practices and the value of reaching consensus. Let us briefly recap the practice of Law, relative to these adherences.

Kincentricity

As the testimonies of Old Arthur and Philip illustrate, the orientation of all life and Law is towards kin, human and non-human. This is shown through the relational linkages which are repeated again and again in their recollections, including references to relationships between people and their non-human ancestors, between husbands and wives, between brothers, fathers and mothers and their children, spirit children and their places of origin, and between people and ceremony. Law has a way of artfully putting into practice relations prefaced on degrees of closeness and distance between people and all parts of Country, achieving a sense of emplacement where everything is at once in relation, but determining also that not just any kind of relation will do.

There is specificity in the connections that are made and the Law ensures that people know their own relationships and how these shape interactions with all other phenomena found in Country. The success of this is that once connection is known, it cannot be denied or disavowed, and if it is, there are corrective steps which can be taken to straighten things up. Because everything in Country is connected through specific lines of descent, this means then that the scope of responsibility does not lie solely with human life or to a person's biological kindred but expands out into a vast world of things and presences to which a person must be responsive. This expands the field of respect and acknowledgement of deep importance to all aspects in Country. Such networks of connection might be understood as nested, like in a 'nested ecology', which distinguishes interrelations between realms, those of the personal, social, environmental, cosmic and spiritual or ancestral (see Wimberley 2009). Yanyuwa know the benefits of these kinds of connections, none more so than the benefits which come from considering relations as necessary to maintain and sustain the order, health and well-being of Country and kin.

Law is a strategy to mitigate against separation, isolation and disconnection. These are considered dangerous states in the Yanyuwa lifeworld, resonating as they do with forms of strangeness and unknowing, threatening ill health for that or those which are unknown, unrelatable, unrecognised and unresponsive. Habits of individuation and selfishness do not thrive within a kincentric world governed by Law. This is why elders work so hard to ensure that people know the Law which keeps them connected and willing to respond to the needs of others in Country.

Empiricism in Country Through Ngalki

Law speaks to and solidifies the empiricism of Country. Country and the places that distinctively mark the land and sea, such as sites of spirit children, or the bodies and marks of ancestral beings (Dreamings), water sources, old time camping sites, burial caves and present-day outstations where families live on their clan Country, exist as the do because of the Law. They were created by the Law, the ancestors, and people's presence there today is determined by rules of kinship, gendered access and familial closeness. In Yanyuwa Law there is absolutely nothing random about the organisation of Country and who moves through it. If behaviour is adopted which does not follow this Law, then the community often undergoes a process of sense-making, dispute resolution and debate as to what has happened, why this has occurred and then what must be done. The business of relating properly to Country is a topic of almost daily discussion in this community.

The character, rhythm and distinctiveness of Country is held as Law by many of the old people and some mid-generation Yanyuwa. Younger Yanyuwa are often still learning the rules, yet through communal debate they are often privy to the tensions which can emerge when Law is not followed. Law can therefore be accessed through conversations and disagreements, some of which take place on social media platforms. Knowledge is actively being transferred each time dispute is raised and consensus reached on what happens next. Underpinning these aspects of Law is the fact that *ngalki* cannot be extinguished, for it is the primal energy and character of Country.

To watch, notice and live with Country that has its own *ngalki* is to have a certain reverence for the land and sea. The integrity of each place matters. This principle is acknowledged by Yanyuwa and by Indigenous peoples all across Australia. The relational modality this inspires is one that has a hugely important role to play in current environmental and ecological crises that face many parts of the world. Law has a way of putting people into much better relations with their world, on terms that make difficult any tendency to destroy, abandon or devalue the environments on which life depends.

The Realpolitik of Law

As discussed in Chap. 2, coming together to talk and work through conflicts and decisions with the aim of reaching consensus is a key political strategy for Yanyuwa. Again, at the basis of this interaction is kin. Yanyuwa often remark on situations where a person has made an individual decision that impacts others, and will comment on the suspiciousness of meetings which are arranged by non-Indigenous visitors (e.g., mining executives, land council representatives, lawyers, school teachers) to speak with a single Yanyuwa person, rather than choosing to follow lines of kinship and speak to groups of bosses for Country. When people are individuated, they are isolated; this might be when a person self-appoints their authority over others, or when they are given priority by outsiders to speak on behalf of the entire community. This often results in political instability. To speak up without having consulted with others is not the realpolitik of Yanyuwa Law.

The realpolitik of Law lies often in refrain, gathering up groups of 'proper' people and acknowledging that knowledge is not freely held, rather is held in accordance with rules that defer to age, clan membership, ceremonial experience, gender and community standing. These aspects of Law are writ large in the events which led to Old Arthur and Philip being the right people to tell their stories of Law to a particular audience and are vividly displayed in the specific events that are detailed in Old Arthur's testimony, involving the actions and choices of mainland and island Rrumburriya bosses. For Philip there were complicating factors which impinged upon his way of telling his Law, largely because of the artifice created by the setting of a land claim hearing overseen by white 'experts' and saturated in a white legal logic. But even amidst these conditions, he navigated his way through a public presentation of Law that retained a commitment to proper practice, deference, consultation, reaching consensus and undertaking collective decision-making before speaking. The way that Yanyuwa navigate and often subvert white structural and relational tendencies is hugely impressive and shows the ways that Law is retained as part of an everyday practice. Law is found in these subtle behaviours and choices.

Law has complexity, that is, an intricacy and people have capacity for negotiation of change and cultural shift. This is a vision of Indigenous cultures and their Laws as highly adept at accommodating, resisting and negotiating the internal, but even more so the external, pressures that distinguish settler colonial and Indigenous relations. Law is not reductionist and in the true nature of realpolitik Old Arthur's and Philip's testimonies showcase the realistic, practical nature of Law that gives consideration to circumstances and factors, rather than strictly binding itself to explicit ideological notions.

In the following chapter we pan back our focus, to return to a discussion of Indigenous Law as more than soft power; more than a 'national asset' to be exploited or engaged in a piecemeal fashion for tourism encounters, creative arts and entertainment. We hope to have painted a rich picture of Yanyuwa Law and realpolitik, and to have thoroughly unsettled any notions of esotericism and ephemerality that might adhere to presentations of Indigenous Laws. Having dedicated our time to Yanyuwa Law in this chapter and Chap. 2, it might be that some readers have questions, particularly concerning how Law might be engaged in the present to strengthen communities, and how global efforts at reworlding Indigenous Law might provide important insights for intercultural politics and healthy communities.

Notes

1. A bush name is a name given to a child by senior kin, often related to actual place names on Country and associated Dreamings. Bush names are often shared with someone of a person's grandparent's generation (see Chap. 2).
2. Yanyuwa have a longstanding tradition of naming watercraft such as canoes. Canoes were given names drawn from the place where they were constructed, from the maker or owner of it, or sometimes from an ancestral being or Dreaming associated with the owner or maker of that canoe (Kearney and Bradley 2015: 172).
3. In the papers of Jean Kirton, a missionary linguist who worked with Yanyuwa and who spent some time at Doomadgee working with Old Arthur, are a number of recorded stories in Yanyuwa that recount details of Old Arthur's childhood and young adulthood on the islands. He spoke with Kirton of the ceremonies that he saw and participated in and often expressed his desire to go back and visit his family at Borroloola.
4. Such was Old Arthur's status as a Yanyuwa Law man connected to Yanyuwa Country that, upon his death and burial in Doomadgee in 1986, some people at that time felt strongly that he should have been brought back to Borroloola to be buried.
5. *Kunabibi* is an enormously important ceremony that has a broad regional focus. It belongs to the Rrumburriya and Mambaliya-Wawukariya groups. The ceremony in particular articulates the ownership of various tracts of land and sea and the Dreamings associated with them. Whilst primarily performed by men, women also have their own ceremonies to perform in association with this ceremony. This ceremony, when performed can bring together very large groups of people from other regional areas such as Doomadgee to the east, Roper River and Numbulwar to the northwest.
6. Old Arthur, Annie a-Karrakayny and Johnson Timothy had urged these two men to attend. This was a highly political, but necessary, move to ensure the acceptance of Lawful processes that had taken place in the past. Both of these men confirmed with Bradley the Lawful truth—*wurrbi* of the events recounted.
7. Note this is also the name of the Old Borroloola Willy who was also present when Old Arthur told this story. It is not unusual for some men and women to have two bushnames. Usually, it is an indicator of seniority, close relationships and ceremonial knowledge.
8. Binbingka were a neighbouring language group to the west of Yanyuwa Country. As a result of colonial violence, Binbingka suffered terribly on the colonial frontier, and today there are no persons who identify as members of this distinct language group and land holding presence in the Gulf of Carpentaria (Roberts 2005; Baker 1999).

9. See a detailed description of *ardirri* in Chap. 2. In the case of Old Arthur's testimony, any child found on another Country such as in this instance could claim to be *wayurungu*, or of 'one water' to the clan group of owning kin.

10. Old Arthur was referring to the time after which colonial presences were formalised in the Borroloola area, coinciding with an increased presence of white residents, white administrators and 'government protectors' who set up a rations depot and welfare outpost, first through the Native Affairs Branch of the Northern Territory Administration and the State Children''s Council and then the Welfare Branch.

11. This area is located within the Victoria River District, Northern Territory, Australia.

12. Yarralin is a remote Aboriginal community in the Northern Territory, also referred to by the name Walangeri. Aboriginal people from several different language groups live today in Yarralin, including Gurindji, Ngaringyman, Bilinara and Mudburra. To date 50,310 hectares of land in and around Yarralin has been returned to Indigenous owners as freehold title under the *Aboriginal Land Rights (Northern Territory) Act 1976* (Australian Government 1976; Northern Land Council 2016: 10).

13. In many instances 'bush courts' will be held for land claim hearings, with judges, court personnel and experts flying into remote communities to hold court at places of significance to the land under claim. These trips are also used for 'site visits' where key places are visited and Indigenous claimant evidence recorded in situ.

14. The *Kundawira* and *Kunumbu* ceremonies were seen to be much more authoritative and powerful than *a-Kunabibi*. It was these two ceremonies that Philip had not seen but was aware of. *Kunumbu* and *Kundawira* were very localised and powerful ceremonies that related to very particular tracts of land and sea under the control of specific Rrumburriya families.

REFERENCES

Adgemis, P. 2017. *We Are Yanyuwa – No Matter What: Town Life, Family and Change*. PhD Thesis, Monash University, Melbourne, Australia.

Akehurst, V. 2006. *A Light in the Darkness: An Anecdotal History of Doomadgee Mission; Fifty-Three Years of Faithful, Fearless Endeavour by Assembly Missionaries*. Malaysia: Selangor.

Australian Government. 1976. *Aboriginal Land Rights (Northern Territory) Act 1976*, No. 191, 1976. Available at: https://www.legislation.gov.au/Details/C2019C00117

Avery, J., and McLaughlin, D. 1977. *Submission by Northern Land Council to the Aboriginal Land Commissioner on the Borroloola Region Land Claim.* Darwin: Northern Land Council.

Baker, R. 1999. *Land Is Life: Continuity Through Change for the Yanyuwa from the Northern Territory of Australia.* Sydney: Allen and Unwin.

Bradley, J. 1992. *Warnarrwarnarr-Barranyi Land Claim.* Darwin: Northern Land Council.

Bradley, J. 2000. *Yanyuwa Sea Country Claim.* Darwin: Northern Land Council.

Bradley, J. 2008. Singing through the sea: Song, sea and emotion. In S. Shaw and Francis (Eds.) *Deep Blue: Critical Reflections on Nature, Religion and Water.* Abingdon, Oxon: Routledge, pp. 17–32.

Bradley, J., with Yanyuwa Families. 2022. *It's Coming from the Times in Front of Us: Country, Kin and the Dugong Hunter Songline.* North Melbourne, Victoria: Australian Scholarly Publishing.

Burke, P. 2011. *Law's Anthropology: From Ethnography to Expert Testimony in Native Title.* Canberra: ANU Press.

Cooke, M. 1995. Interpreting in a cross-cultural cross-examination: An Aboriginal case study. *International Journal of the Sociology of Language* 113: 99–112.

Glaskin, K. 2017. *Crosscurrents: Law and Society in a Native Title Claim to Land and Sea.* Western Australia: UWA Press.

Kearney, A. 2018. Returning to that which was never lost: Indigenous Australian saltwater identities, a history of Australian land claims and the paradox of return. *History and Anthropology* 29(2): 184–203. https://doi.org/10.108 0/02757206.2017.1397646

Kearney, A. 2021. *Keeping Company: An Anthropology of Being-In-Relation.* Abingdon, Oxfordshire: Routledge.

Kearney, A. 2022. 'The law has changed, and you can get some of your land back…': Aboriginal land rights, subjection and the law. In P. Cane, L. Ford, and M. McMillan (Eds.) *The Cambridge Legal History of Australia.* Cambridge: Cambridge University Press, pp. 354–376.

Kearney, A., and Bradley, J. 2015. When a long way in a bark canoe becomes a quick trip in a boat: Changing relationships to sea country & Yanyuwa watercraft technology. *Quaternary International* 385: 166–176. https://doi.org/10.1016/j.quaint.2014.07.004

Kirton, J. 1965–1968. Unpublished field journals and Yanyuwa language transcriptions.

Martin, R., and Trigger, D. 2015. Negotiating belonging: Plants, people, and indigeneity in northern Australia. *The Journal of the Royal Anthropological Institute* 21(2): 276–295. https://doi.org/10.1111/1467-9655.12206

Nash, D., and Henderson, J. (Eds.) 2002. *Language in Native Title.* Canberra: Aboriginal Studies Press.

Niranjana, T. 1998. Feminism and translation in India: Contexts, politics, futures. *Cultural Dynamics* 10(2): 133–146.

Roberts, T. 2005. *Frontier Justice: A History of the Gulf Country to 1900*. St Lucia, QLD: University of Queensland Press.

Rose, D. B. 1995. *Women and Land Claims*. Issues paper, Australian Institute of Aboriginal and Torres Strait Islanders Studies. Canberra: Native Title Research Unit.

Rose, D. B. 1996. Land rights and deep colonising: The erasure of women. *Aboriginal Law Bulletin* 3(85): 6.

Rose, D. B. 2000. *Dingo Makes Us Human: Life and Land in Australian Aboriginal Culture*. Cambridge: Cambridge University Press.

Seton, K., and Bradley, J. 2005. Self-determination or 'deep colonising'. In Hocking (Ed.) *Unfinished Constitutional Business*. Canberra: Aboriginal Studies Press, pp. 32–46.

Sutton, P. 2003. *Native Title in Australia*. Cambridge: Cambridge University Press.

Toohey, J. 1979. *Borroloola Land Claim*. Canberra: Australian Government Publishing.

Toussaint, S., Tonkinson, M., and Trigger, D. 2001. Gendered landscapes: The politics and processes of inquiry and negotiating interests in land. In P. Brock (Ed.) *Words and Silences: Aboriginal Women, Politics and Land*. London: Routledge, pp. 157–174.

Trigger, D. 1992. *Whitefella Comin': Aboriginal Responses to Colonialism in Northern Australia*. New York: Cambridge University Press.

Trigger, D. 2004. Anthropology in Native Title court cases: 'Mere pleading, expert opinion, or hearsay'. In S. Toussaint (Ed.) *Crossing Boundaries: Cultural, Legal, Historical & Practice Issues in Native Title*. Melbourne: Melbourne University Press, pp. 24–33.

Trigger, D., Martin, D., Memmott, P., Winn, P., Burke, P., Peterson, N., Veth, P., Holcombe, S., and Palmer, K. 2013. Forensic social anthropology. In I. Freckelton and H. Selby (Eds.) *Expert Evidence: Law, Practice, Procedure and Advocacy*. Sydney: Thomson Reuters, pp. 36–51.

Vázquez, R. 2011. Translation as erasure: Thoughts on Modernity's epistemic violence. *Journal of Historical Sociology* 24(1): 27–44. https://doi.org/10.1111/j.1467-6443.2011.01387.x

Walsh, M. 2008. Which way? Difficult options for vulnerable witnesses in Australian Aboriginal land claim and Native Title cases. *Journal of English Linguistics* 36(3): 239–265. https://doi.org/10.1177/0075424208321142

Walsh, M. 2011. A neo-colonial farce? Discourses of deficit in Australian Aboriginal land claim and Native Title cases. In C. Candling and J. Crichton (Eds.) *Discourses of Deficit*. Basingstoke: Palgrave Macmillan, pp. 327–346.

Wimberley, E. 2009. *Nested Ecology: The Place of Humans in the Ecological Hierarchy.* Baltimore: John Hopkins University Press.

Young, A. 2009. *Jealous for Country: A Short Legal History of the Attempts of Government and Miners to Obtain and Consolidate Control of the Natural Resources of the McArthur River Region and the Continuing Resistance of the Yanyuwa, Gurdanji and Garawa People.* Available at: http://williamforster. com/wp-content/uploads/2008/11/Article-McArthur-River-Jealous-for-Our-Country-TY-13.04.101.pdf

CHAPTER 4

More Than Soft Power

Abstract In this chapter we take the discussion of Indigenous Law further, by exploring the problematic notion of soft power and examining the epistemic logics and bad habits that have led to a perception of Indigenous Laws and knowledges as marginal, esoteric and mystical. It is argued that the positioning of Indigenous Law as an esoteric or subordinate alternative to contemporary white liberal democracy is a framing which substantiates a deep inequity between Indigenous and non-Indigenous peoples and communities.

Problematising the interface at which Indigenous Laws meets western bureaucratic and legal habits is however only one part of this chapter. It is crucial to retain our focus on Indigenous Laws as they are lived and held by people within their own communal contexts. Hence the chapter importantly attends to the positioning on Indigenous Laws in contemporary life, placing an emphasis on the role of Law in supporting communities, amidst the changing conditions and contexts in which Law is emplaced. We explore the overarching applications of Indigenous Laws *for Indigenous benefit*.

Keywords Soft power critique • Stakeholder peril • Reworlding Law • Pluralism • Indigenous benefit • Yanyuwa Lawfulness

© The Author(s) 2023

A. Kearney et al., *Indigenous Law and the Politics of Kincentricity and Orality*, https://doi.org/10.1007/978-3-031-19239-5_4

In this book we have sought to convey, through direct testimonies and ethnographic accounts, the influence and power of Indigenous Law as it is emplaced in Yanyuwa Country. On the basis of observations and lived experiences with Law in action, we also contend that Indigenous Laws more broadly are structured bodies of knowledge and praxis that have an important place in the lives of their practitioners today and thus exert influence over the lands, waters and peoples for whom they inform aspects of life. This is a distinctive shift away from ideas of Law as esoteric or somehow mystical and imaginary, lost in translation to outsider audiences and often represented as stories and folklore. The folkloric hangover of positioning Indigenous Laws as soft knowledge, soft assets or soft power is the implication of traditionality, irrationality and pre-modernity. The failing of these presumptions is an inability to fully recognise the importance of Law. Such a tendency limits the inclusion of Indigenous knowledges in wider intellectual, political, social and economic life, denying Law a deeper influence in collective decision-making and governmental or western legal/bureaucratic interventions which directly impact upon and shape Indigenous people's lives.

Yanyuwa families have lived through many experiences in which their Law has been overlooked, sidelined through western political and legal dominance or simply misunderstood. Few people outside of this community have taken the time to acknowledge the Law for Yanyuwa Country in the southwest Gulf of Carpentaria or to learn aspects of Law as they structure and organise everyday life. Some of the most prevalent fields across which Law structures everyday life include, for example, kinship and lines of descent, family and household makeup, parental and adoptive/carer rights, land and sea management as orchestrated through clan ownership and ancestral responsibility, rules of access and knowledge sharing. The expansiveness of Law also extends into knowledge of species habits, ecological integrity and community governance as actioned through specific decision-making processes, including a reliance on consensus and hyper-relationality, and particular expressions of dissent and conflict resolution. It has been our intention to share with the reader the complexity and sophistication with which Yanyuwa Law is enacted and held as part of a contemporary world.

In this chapter we take the discussion of Indigenous Law further, by exploring the problematic notion of soft power and examining the epistemic logics and bad habits that have led to a perception of Indigenous Laws and knowledges as marginal, esoteric and mystical. It is argued that the positioning of Indigenous Law as an esoteric or subordinate alternative to contemporary white liberal democracy is a framing which substantiates a deep inequity between Indigenous and non-Indigenous peoples and communities. This framing creates the conditions which spur the use and maintenance of categories such as 'stakeholder'. Stakeholder status, we argue, creates peril for Indigenous knowledge holders and Law practitioners in a number of ways, and this can be readily observed in a range of contexts and intercultural encounters, as experienced by Yanyuwa.

Problematising the interface at which Indigenous Laws meet western bureaucratic and legal habits is however only one part of this chapter. It is crucial to retain our focus on Indigenous Laws as they are lived and held by people within their own communities. Hence the remaining parts of this chapter will attend to the positioning on Indigenous Laws in contemporary life, placing an emphasis on the role of Law in supporting communities, amidst the changing conditions and contexts in which Law is emplaced. We thus explore the overarching applications of Indigenous Laws *for Indigenous benefit*. One point of extension in this discussion of benefit, which involves non-Indigenous interests, is the call for the recognition of political pluralism, for this will have implications for the future of legal, social and political processes in settler colonial contexts which effect Indigenous peoples' lives.

The Problem with Soft Power

Indigenous knowledges are increasingly recognised for their role in providing pathways towards mitigating global crises, specifically those associated with environment and climate change (e.g., Kulnieks et al. 2013; Nader 1996; Nelson and Shilling 2018; Ridgeway and Jacques 2015; Williams 2021). Even a cursory read of the literature reveals an enthusiasm towards Indigenous knowledges within western empirical and social sciences that is unparalleled in recent decades. Yet the vast majority of interactions with and applications of Indigenous knowledges to scientific and societal problems fail to mention Indigenous Laws as underpinning said knowledge. Yet this book has shown that knowledge operates through a paradigm of Law, thus highlighting that one does not exist without the other. Perhaps in the broader field of engagement with Indigenous knowledge, there is a reluctance to invoke notions of Law in sequence with knowledge, for to do so is to politicise knowledge and raise consciousness of the many systems of rules, regulations, procedures and expected behaviours that may adhere to the praxis of Indigenous knowledge.

The separation of knowledge from Law is what allows Indigenous knowledges to be treated (by governments, researchers, tourists and other non-practitioners) as soft assets, intangible and of indeterminate value. In a typical and economically reductionist sense, soft assets have little or no market value, or physical form. Soft assets carry soft power, that is, the ability to co-opt (integrate into and compound with the whole), rather than coerce (constrain, force or compel), as is the case with hard power. For Indigenous knowledge trapped in this frame of reference, it is marketability and appeal to outsiders which dominates and recognition becomes dependent on a vision of unwavering esotericism and tradition. Knowledge is thus packaged as a 'feel good' decolonial option, showcased as an embrace of alternative forms of insight and taken up by outsiders through stories, ceremonies and songs. Oral traditions, rendered as soft forms of insight, are rarely described as overtly political, economically important forms of deep intellectualism or diplomacy.

Carpenter and Tsykarev (2021) describe recent international Indigenous diplomacy efforts concerning human rights and the UN Declaration on the Rights of Indigenous Peoples. They (2021:118) describe a situation in which states are "relinquishing some 'soft power' space to non-state actors", namely, Indigenous peoples in diplomacy efforts on the world stage, and specifically in developments at the United Nations. They explain "the role of Indigenous Peoples in international diplomacy and particularly human rights diplomacy [as] both distinctive and important". Clarification is given as to the origins and roots of this diplomacy, which is described briefly as Law—based on traditions and the regulation of external relationships. It is on matters of climate change and biodiversity that "Indigenous Peoples are showing their capacity to bring a more capacious approach to human rights and the potential for enhancing global well-being". Whilst indicating a more progressive platform for Indigenous participation in the UN global context, there remains a marginality in this presence, in its positioning as an alternative political vision, granted space by the occupying centre (a reluctantly relinquishing state in many cases) to address matters of well-being rather than politics. This alternative political vision is not received as a coercive presence and in fact is juxtaposed by reference to 'heavier' diplomatic tools, possessed by the state. Rather, its presence is envisioned by state powers as advisory, a performance of cultural norms and practices and spiritual attachments within a stage show of highly normative diplomatic rhetoric which is rarely described as cultural, spiritual or ideological. State power is universally depicted as authoritative, encompassing and tacit.

Carpenter and Tsykarev (2021:122) openly discuss the constraining presence of state dominance, the ignorance towards and exploitation of issues of security and economics as they impact Indigenous peoples' lives, and tensions among Indigenous groups on the basis of differing political worldviews. These pressures conspire to relinquish Indigenous Laws a soft power, an optional diplomatic tool rarely taken up and only granted an audience at the discretionary interest and power of the state. Similarly, the 2019 celebration of Indigenous knowledge as a soft power asset by the Australian Department of Foreign Affairs and Trade is a striking illustration of the soft asset logic and soft power discourse as it also constrains deeper understandings and democratic dealings with Indigenous knowledge holders and their Law.

> Some of Australia's best soft power assets are outside of government and we want to make sure we draw on diverse Australian perspectives from a broad cross-section of the community.

> This includes Indigenous leaders in culture and the arts, science, business and sport who promote Australia's soft power every day in their work, including through their partnerships with businesses, individuals and creatives in other countries (Australian Government, Department of Foreign Affairs and Trade 2019).[1]

This goes so far as to position actual persons—Indigenous leaders—as soft assets in the mind of the colonial polity, a strangely dehumanising notion that depoliticises people, their knowledge and Law. There is a degree of emptiness in this DFAT statement, which surely induces a frustration for Indigenous peoples and insults the integrity of their Laws and leaders in a national context where Indigenous peoples are the most politically under-represented, the most incarcerated and most impoverished of citizens. The take home message of the Australian Commonwealth government is thus a warm and soft rhetoric of feel-good mentions of Indigenous presence, Laws, knowledges and imperatives, in the face of a multitude of denials of rights, recognition and reparation. The reverberating point is that Indigenous Laws are not being taken seriously.

For Yanyuwa, and many Indigenous groups, knowledge is not free, rather it is to be governed by Law—principles, codes and relational expectations in how it is applied. These covenants, in accordance with rules, are to some extent negotiable in time and context, but they are not transposable. The tendency to exploit Indigenous knowledge in isolation from its Law, as a practice of external and piecemeal engagement without adhering to the contextual rules which govern the formation and sharing of knowledge, relies upon a suite of presumptions concerning the nature of intellectualism and property. It also invokes and reinforces concepts such as custodianship and stewardship, which dominate frameworks for mainstream understandings of the ways in which Law is held by Indigenous groups and individuals. Custodianship and stewardship misstep the exclusive authority which is inherent in Indigenous Laws as they are emplaced, and also undermine realities of ownership, exclusive possession, authority and rights to control access. The west's ideal of knowledge is that it can be generalised into abstractions of this kind, and thus constituted beyond intersubjective agreement. The definition of a steward is, according to dictionary entry, to manage or look after another's property. If we are to accept that Indigenous people are stewards, then for whom are they looking after Country? The implicit assumption is that the lands and waters were waiting for European colonists and their aggressive takeover. As Graham Friday Dimanyurru grappled,

> Alright I go out to my Country, out to my mother's Country and everywhere I look I see white people, having a good time. Are they looking after Country? They have no idea, they just go about freely like they are now the owners. Where does his white law come from? What about my Law? When do we get to say our Law is what holds this Country? Maybe then we can stop worrying so much.

In many respects, all of these terms—custodian, steward, tradition, stakeholder—are all soft positionings developed by white legal practitioners because western law cannot negotiate or incorporate the complex web of relationships, obligations and responsibilities held by Yanyuwa Law. And yet because of the power of western legal frameworks and guiding principles, Indigenous peoples are forced into using these soft options to explain their own Law in public forums and meetings. For Yanyuwa this most often occurs in meetings which involve speaking about their Country (e.g., meetings on matters of land and sea rights, natural resource management, prospecting and mining). As author Mavis Timothy a-Muluwamara often says, in meetings where these kinds of terms or categories are insisted upon by bureaucrats, "We don't think like that, and we don't speak like that".

For Yanyuwa, neither custodianship nor stewardship adequately describe their relationship to Law, Country and knowledge. Both terms position the human at a distance from the lifeworld in which they operate (a custodian 'takes care', while a steward 'manages'), and both rely upon a degree of separation of the human from other forms of life, while failing to articulate the sense of innate kincentric bond that comes with hyper-relationality as the primal orientations for ancestrally based Law. When modalities of relating are distinguished by a kincentricity that brings together all forms of life, there can be no exclusivity in the role of the human nor a denial of the relational push and pull which keeps Law operating. It is the actuality of kincentricity which drives Yanyuwa efforts at land and sea restitution and which motivates the continuous pursuit, through all available channels, to safeguard their exclusive rights to Country, even if this requires having to entertain and participate in a white legal system which contests and challenges Indigenous principles at each turn.

It is therefore our contention that the language of soft power, soft assets, custodianship and stewardship all severely undermines Indigenous Law and operates to marginalise and delegitimise Indigenous claims to lands and waters, and autonomous legal, political and ethical regimes. Rocks, trees, watercourses, hills, ranges, sea, reefs, sandbars, sea grass beds, fish, birds, reptiles, all living things and phenomena are impregnated with consciously held meanings, events, stories and songs which are held by men and women. Law then is a biological and geographical literacy that can take years to fully acquire and comprehend.

The first step in educating wider audiences on the nature of Indigenous Law is to raise awareness of the many Laws which exist, beyond those of the west. This is an exercise in ontological expansion, an unflattening of the knowledge field which is commonly referred to as 'the law' (see Kearney 2021). Multiplying realities or potentials in how Law is understood is crucial to an embrace of plurality, a disposition which offsets the unfortunate tendency of the west to flatten human existence into a single conception of knowledge and law. The second step is to switch out the soft power discourse for one which relies more appropriately on articulations of complexity, rigor, political flair, structural integrity and widespread influence. So too we argue for a rhetoric of utility and action as linked to Indigenous Laws and the knowledge practices they support.

Together, as the Yanyuwa and non-Indigenous authors of this book, we have developed a list of recommendations on how outsiders might begin to engage more ethically and expansively with Indigenous Laws and knowledges. These have emerged over decades of sharing and discussing matters of Law in the Yanyuwa lifeworld and beyond. They are based on experience and past and present shortcomings in the spaces in which Indigenous knowledge is increasingly being taken. Yanyuwa specifications for respectful and ethical encounters with Law include realising the following,

> Indigenous knowledge is held in accordance with Law and the two cannot be separated.
> No knowledge is outside of the Law and access to knowledge and Law is controlled.
> Law is emplaced and specific to context and time, thus it pays to know something of the history and contemporary conditions which inform Law in the present moment.
> Law and knowledge are responsive and can change over time. Tradition and romanticism undermine the power and flexibility of Law.
> Outsider engagements with Law must recognise that Law operates through relationships between human, non-human and non-living entities.
> The centrality of western knowledge and law is an artefact of history and contemporary circumstances derived of coloniality. It is not a natural event.
> Indigenous Laws and knowledges are rigorous, nested into a rich field of politics and social life and follow logics and structures.
> Encounters with Indigenous Laws and knowledges require time. The formation of strong relationships is essential to ethical engagements.
> Indigenous people own their lands and waters, Law and knowledge.

Woven through these Yanyuwa specifications is an imperative for permissions. This includes permission to know, and one must be able to articulate how one came to know whatever Law is being talked about, as Dinah Norman a-Marrngawi and her sister Annie a-Karrakayny explain below. As a preface, their conversation (below) occurred at a particularly intense time for the Yanyuwa community. A self-proclaimed white 'discoverer' and voyager named Ben Cropp had published photos of an extremely important sacred site in the Pellew Islands. The site was a series of burial caves, where the bones of deceased Wuyaliya kin were interred in sacred hollow log burial coffins (*larla*). In the photos, Cropp's wife is shown removing bones from the log coffin of Dinah's father. There was much distress in the community about this event and a lot of talk about how the Law functioned. This conversation is part of what Dinah, Annie and other women spoke of at the time. This was in 1985. Cropp's (1980) images were published in 1980 and the contents had only been made known to Yanyuwa families in early 1985.

Annie: People never went free, you had to know the Law, you had to be able to talk to that Law.

Dinah: You have to be able to say where did you find that Law, what ceremony you have seen, what songs you have in your mouth, what man and what women let you talk.

Annie: Like we say it like this, I can talk because my mother's father gave me eyes to see the Law, or you might say I can talk like this because my father's father gave me ears to hear.

Dinah: You just can't go free, someone had to give you the Law, show the Law, show you the Country where that Law came from, let you listen to the songs that hold the Country, hold the Law.

Annie: That's the way we learn, that's where permission comes from, you have to have permission, if you have no permission, you have no Law for the Country, you just remain ignorant.

Dinah: And then you got no authority.

Annie: And how is this, I have seen this, any white fella can come along and say he has authority because he has law, law from a book, they still don't know anything for Country.

Dinah: We two are here, we are proper Law women because we were given eyes to see and ears to hear properly. This is not a little thing.

Annie: Yes, right people, right family, right Country.

Dinah: It's not a little thing, if you call the name of the Country, you have to be able to say who gave you that name, call the name of a ceremony, call the name of old people, people will say, where did you learn that, who gave you those things.

Annie: This is no little thing, this is the big story, I can talk li-*wankala karnalu-ŋgunda ŋgarna-mi, karnalu-ŋgunda ŋgarna-anma ŋaninya barra narnu-yuwa*– the old people gave me eyes to see they gave me ears to hear, this the Law (1985).

There is embedded in this discussion a distinction of Law as both intellectual and sensual; it is embodied and enacted, but in accordance with rules and appropriate timings throughout the life course. There is such rigour in how a person comes to know Law and operate as a lawful person. This point is crucial to an understanding of Yanyuwa Law yet remains a highly contested fact when Yanyuwa encounter the legal systems of the settler state, which render lawful persons as partial and answerable to another, often incommensurable system of white law and governance. In the specific example of land rights claims and general land restitution matters, the centrality of Yanyuwa Law is displaced as people are funnelled through a legal system which renders them 'claimants' and 'stakeholders'.

Most detrimental to the rights and well-being of Indigenous peoples has been the imposition of this status of stakeholder, a role which is determined and played out in a white legal arena. Stakeholder status denies the centrality of Indigenous Laws and presumes a relational contract in which all parties are treated as equal. Time has shown that this is not the case and to presume so ignores the ontological and epistemic drive that distinguishes coloniality.

THE PERIL OF STAKEHOLDER STATUS

Stakeholder status relies upon particular configurations of power and terms of relating. It operates from a competitive logic determined by those who have power. The settler state holds power and creates 'stakeholders', a composite of parties held to be of equal form and function. Stakeholder analysis places an issue or problem at the conceptual centre. The criteria and method by which entities, people and communities are deemed to have a 'stake' in that central issue or problem are riddled with the prevailing logic of coloniality as enacted through colonial conditions, habits and structures. Of coloniality, Grosfoguel (2005:115) writes, "we live in a world in which relations between cultures are vertical, between dominated and dominators, colonized and colonizers". This reality inspires bad relations and a suite of "privileges—won through the exploitation and domination of global coloniality" (Grosfoguel 2005: 115). There are deep inequalities of power that trace their roots and routes to the "complicity of the north in the south's exploitation" (Grosfoguel 2005: 115), and these settle into forms of discourse and action.

For Yanyuwa, stakeholder status has always brought dispossessing qualities, a reality directly attributable to the colonial underpinnings which centralise white authority and political dominance and determine the right of 'others' to participate. This effect becomes evident not only through Indigenous participation in the legislative land rights process but also through a suite of other encounters with the west's proclaimed democratic decision-making processes which come to dominate Indigenous people's involvements in land and sea management protocols and practices, educational reform, community governance and even healthcare. For Yanyuwa, specific matters that are closely associated with their Law and ways of knowing, and which are routinely obstructed include, for example, the regular burning of Country to maintain ecological and cultural health, the placing of objects of significance onto Country (such as the personal items of deceased kin which are bundled up and placed on their ancestral Country and other ritual practices), and the protection of certain sites and areas so that resource extractors, tourists and other non-Yanyuwa visitors will not disturb these important places associated with the travels and bodies of Dreaming ancestors.

It is an afront for Yanyuwa that outsiders who are ignorant of Yanyuwa Law can move freely around their Country and make decisions which place restrictions on Yanyuwa activity and actions. As Dinah Norman a-Marrngawi exclaimed, back in 1986 (when tourism was on the rise across her Country),

> It is wrong, these strangers to this Country, these people that have no emotion for this Country. Tourists just go where they want, as they please, they disturb the sacred places, the burial grounds of our ancestors, the places that are held by strong Law. They disturb these places without thinking and then they go, and they leave behind for us, a very troubled and argumentative place. We are blaming each other for the trouble but we did not make this trouble, but we are left to make things right again, these strangers just walk free, over and over again.

In the stakeholder business of white law and governance, Indigenous Law becomes a conversation piece, a negotiation point. The stakeholder approach carries rudimentary democratic aesthetics and as such is conventionally perceived as a universally applicable 'grassroots' decision-making process that can only lead to fairer outcomes—where all parties with an 'interest' in an issue are brought together to have their stake assessed and balanced in the making of decisions. However, like many liberal or rights-based approaches, being rendered as a mere stakeholder in forums which inculcate historical illiteracy, cultural incompetence and blindness to power imbalances leads to Indigenous peoples being misunderstood and sidelined. Several of the authors of this book have sat on plans of management boards, and sacred site protection boards. They have launched and participated in land claims, native title and other restitutional and compensatory processes, and sought to negotiate the intricacies of cultural recognition and rights in the pursuit of better schooling for their young people, equitable healthcare services in their remote community and representation for family members who are incarcerated in prison. Too often they arrive at such crucial discussions, which directly concern the needs of their community and family members, only to be relegated to the role of stakeholder, an act and position which is offensive and handicaps their fullest participation.

One of the most pervasive colonial deceits is the positioning of Indigenous people as mere stakeholders in their own Country. This process of decision-making renders all interests equal in negotiations about Indigenous lands and waters, communal interests and well-being. Out on the so-called level playing field, where a bevy of stakeholders gather, we find a ground fractured into isolated, interchangeable, comparable units that are all said to have equal rights and interests. This imaginary setting purports to offer perfect competition and perfect choice, such that the participants themselves are substitutable because they have no history, no culture, no familial or community ties and no commitments (other than to themselves as agents of material self-interest). Part of the deceitfulness lies in the demonstrable fact that when it comes to inequality, people's histories and cultures do matter.

> Graham Friday Dimanyurru: It's like they think we have no family, no Country, no ceremony, that we are just the same as whitefellas. From what I can see whitefella is lost, so he just wants everyone to be like him. When they gonna grow ears [meaning gather some intelligence] and just listen to us for a change, you know really understand. This meeting business all the time and this stakeholder talking is just trying to bring us down.

Graham's response was in relation to a meeting of 'stakeholders' who had gathered to discuss a large mining port facility that stands on Yanyuwa Country. This port facility is linked to further inland mining operations controlled by Glencore Mining, which operates on Yanyuwa and Gudanji land in the southwest Gulf of Carpentaria. The port facility is located at a place locally referred to as Bing Bong which is on Yanyuwa Country, and the site is constituted under western law as excised pastoral land, held under lease by Glencore. Graham's remarks came in the wake of the meeting (held in 2009), at which a significant amount of time and attention was given to describing the roles and interests of various 'stakeholders' who had gathered to discuss future plans for mining operations on Yanyuwa and Gudanji Country. It was explained by mining executives that there were 'multiple stakeholders', each of whom had a right to be in attendance at this meeting and who also had equal rights to speak about the land and sea under consideration. The meeting however became a staging ground for a much larger 'white discussion' about needs and aspirations for the port facility, as articulated by Glencore Mining executives.

Along with masking the tensions and violent histories which have given rise to profound social inequalities for Indigenous Australians, the superficial level playing field which is imposed through a stakeholder rhetoric also neutralises ethics. It creates, in effect, a human gravel pit—a ground of fragments within which there are no actual selves in relationship with others or particular histories and present realities which shape the relational context, but only isolated units among whom ethics and ethical relational encounters may be possible (not withstanding willingness and histories of failing to do so on the behalf of those in power). In short, the unmaking of distinctions cuts across the relationships which give rise to ethics, leaving wounded remnants whose purposes and meanings are being erased.

This battleground is the mythical middle ground, and it has been the most brutal for Indigenous, First Nations people. It is through a performance of objectivity, a trait deemed exclusive to white people, that the power of race is sustained to mark difference and to subjugate. An illustration of this comes from the recollection of an event involving Annie a-Karrakayny. This took place in August 1995 at a very intense meeting of 'stakeholders', which had been convened after 30 dugongs had been killed by professional fishing nets one night on Yanyuwa Country. The meeting had brought together Yanyuwa community leaders, representatives from the government fisheries department and the Northern Land Council,[2] and the fishermen responsible for the mass drowning.

Annie did not like the way the meeting was going so she said to the group, "Look I just need to say this, all you white men, we are not dealing with a little animal, we are talking about dugong. In our Law, in our way of thinking this animal is a big man, a proper Lawful being, we have to talk carefully". The response to Annie from the chairman of the meeting was along the lines of, "thank you, but we have to talk about important issues here". Annie later recalled that this dismissal had left her feeling "so shamed by those white people". She went on to say:

> The Law for this Country is now low down. How is it possible to lift up the Law for the Country, for the dugong again? I am so shamed, *karnamba-wajkirrala* (I will hide myself away). Whitefella made this trouble, but trouble comes to us Yanyuwa people too, people will start blaming each other, *jungkayi* and *ngimirringki* will argue with each other. All the people for the Dugong Dreaming will be arguing, and whitefella that made the trouble walks away free, just like nothing ever happened.

Also impacted by the events of this meeting and deeply hurt by the shocking lack of remorse and care for the dead dugong and by extension their Yanyuwa kin, Dinah Norman a-Marrngawi pleaded with her audience of listeners at the meeting on this day to understand the gravity of the situation,

> This Country is low down now [it is grieving]. There is stink all over the Country. How are we going to lift this place up again [emotionally engage with it]. There will be a lot of argument, the Law is hard, it is tough, whitefella just does not know.

Dinah's brother, Billy Miller Rijirmgu, also grappled to make sense of the deaths, drawing on Law and the flow of responsibilities between human and non-human kin to compile some sort of understanding as to what this event might mean for the present and future of Yanyuwa Country,

> So you tell me what's going to happen now? All those dugongs are dead, just floating around...You know what's going to happen? All the other dugong are going to clear out, you can't kill that many and reckon they are going to stay. Just like when we cook dugong wrong way, or hunt dugong wrong way, that dugong go, that dugong is there thinking, there is no Law

left in this Country. So they go, they go somewhere else and they look back, then they might think, aaah there is Law coming back into that Country, those people have straightened themselves up, we can go back now.

STRAIGHTENING THINGS UP

As outlined in Chap. 2, *narnu-Yuwa*, Yanyuwa lawfulness, is often introduced as *Yanyuwangala*. *Yanyuwangala* is the knowledge, beliefs customs, practices, rules and regulations of the Yanyuwa way of life. It may include rules of who can marry who, or the principles of land tenure as well as ethical and moral edicts such as "don't steal another person's property or don't travel and hunt without permission on someone else's clan Country". In this respect the Law fulfils many of the same function as western culture's criminal and civil law as well as the practices, ethics and codes of behaviour established by mainstream civil and religious institutions.

The Law is vast and expansive and also fulfils the role taken up by mainstream culture's body of scientific knowledge, in that it explains the proper functioning of the world, of Country in geographical, ecological and biological terms. For example, it is Law that prescribes the understanding that certain fruits such as the cycad palm nuts will be ripe at a certain time of the year. It is also the Law for this species that it belongs to people of the Rrumburriya clan, that it must be processed in particular ways and that it was a fruit that could be harvested in huge quantities to support large gatherings of people for ceremonial activity. It is also a fruit that traces its Law to the Tiger Shark Dreaming ancestor and the *Ngabaya*—Spirit Man Dreaming ancestor. For Yanyuwa the Law is the reference point for direction about how *all* things live in the world, not only the human presences. "The Law is like a road deep in the ground, the Law is a big thing, serious" Annie a-Karrakayny (1992). Law is not a soft option, it gives status, it is hard to learn and people who do learn are worthy of respect such as 'professor in universities' (Annie a-Karrakayny 1996).

To write of Law today is to find a balance in the lived experiences of elders for whom Law was their foundational experience and learning, and the experiences of younger generations for whom the acquisition of knowledge through the framework of Law has been very different. In the preparation of this book, it was put to the authors (by a reviewer) that we might consider reflecting on the reworlding of Indigenous knowledges and Laws in the present moment. This was not a language or concept that we had chosen to engage with for the purpose of this story; however, we have explored its relevance and wish to comment on the specificity of what safeguarding Law involves and to reflect on how the straightening up of Law is an important part of ensuring its ongoing practice.

Reworlding appears, in a more general sense, to describe a process of revitalisation and re-presencing of some form of knowledge or practice in the present moment, possibly in a different place. In the case of Indigenous Laws and knowledges, it is presumed that reworlding occurs because of an intrinsic drive and determination of merit and value. And it operates out from the principle that the intellectualism and praxis of Law and knowledge has relevancy in the world today. However, where we are uncertain of the efficacy of this expression reworlding to describe the Yanyuwa context of Law in the present is the reference to 'worlding'. Re – is taken to mean some form of return, re-inscription, re-presencing, reviving or re-thinking, a paradigm shift in time and space—locating relevance within a 'world', potentially one different to a worldly context in which something has previously existed.

Reworlding involves a concerted effort to reimagine the present moment and what it contains, as places, spaces, knowledges and all range of possible presences. By reworlding we are generating a multiplicity of contextual futures to affect the present positively. Reworlding takes the notion of world-building as a radical tool to instigate change in the world. One of the first attempts by Yanyuwa to reworld their Law came in 1996. At the time, John Bradley had asked elders what it was that they wanted to do with all of the collected material they had been documenting together. This included *kujika*, stories, ancestral narratives, language and ceremonial details. They said, "we want maps, we want all the Yanyuwa names, we need them so young people can know". Thus over a period of three years and many meetings, the Yanyuwa visual atlas came into existence (see Yanyuwa et al. 2003). It is a visual and Yanyuwa-centric mapping of their sea Country, in accordance with its Law. Its creation was a radical discontinuity from orality to written form, from physical geography to a world of specially worked maps. It remains in circulation among the families and is used widely in teaching at the local school and in all range of cultural and resource management contexts and discussions.

Kathleen Stewart (2010) provides a definition of worlding referring to the 'affective nature' of the world in which 'non-human agency', comprising 'forms, rhythms and refrains' (for example), reaches a point of 'expressivity' for an individual and develops a sense of 'legibility'. Through this process a particular world emerges for the individual through their engagement with a number of interrelated phenomena. Anderson and Harrison (2010:8) expand on worlding further: "...the term 'world' does not refer to an extant thing but rather the context or background against which particular things show up and take on significance: a mobile but more or less stable ensemble of practices, involvements, relations, capacities, tendencies and affordances".

The culture of Law that forms the Yanyuwa lifeworld is itself given by ancestral beings and is maintained by Yanyuwa men and women, thus constituting a worlding. Thus, it has two contexts in which it operates, and a vastly configured world from which it emerges and sustains. It is at once of the ancestral realm, sentient and present in all aspects of Country and kin, and also present in the daily decisions, relations and conduct of Yanyuwa across their multi-generational community, held and understood in a number of ways. The culture of the Law itself is of the Country, from the Country and in certain ceremonial contexts symbolic of Country. Country, people and Law exist together, one does not exist without the other. Such a view grounds the process of Law in very practical ways so that it creates a nexus of rights grounded in mutual equality. In the governance and day-to-day decision-making that shapes life, concerns for Country must be considered, people must be considered, species and relationships must be considered, and all things then are of the Law.

If any discussion of reworlding is to hold and speak relevance to the continued practice of Yanyuwa Law, then this nexus of meaning and practice must be taken into consideration and there must be some commentary as to the very notion of the world into which reworlding occurs. In many respects, because Law is given by ancestral beings, it can never be reworlded, because it is always in and of the Yanyuwa lifeworld, due to the prevailing sentiency and endurance of these ancestral presences in Country. What can be reworlded though is the manner in which Yanyuwa men and women across generations maintain their Law. This is to speak of reworlding as re-presencing, or as Yanyuwa describe it, *straightening up* and continuing to hold the Law.

Yanyuwa will often use the expression 'to straighten up', in an effort to convey the strains and efforts required in redressing the path of something that has been interrupted, misdirected or become potentially lost.

To straighten up is to set things right, to follow the proper way, and in the case of Law is to follow the path of *Yanyuwangala*, or the *a-yabala* (path, or road). This is the path of ancestral beings who placed meaning and order into Country. This is a path of deeper meaning. How people strive to straighten up the Law in the contemporary scene of life in Borroloola is multifaceted, enduringly creative and heavily policed. For example, a group of young men working hard to relearn an intricate *kujka* (songline) associated with the *a-Marndiwa* ceremony (a ceremony dedicated to boy's initiation into young manhood) do so in order for this ceremony to be maintained, and to prevent it being lost as elders pass on and language decline becomes perilous.[3] But their process of learning is different to how their elders came to learn and participate in this ceremony. They work closely with John Bradley, who has recorded *kujika* for over four decades with Yanyuwa elders.

These young song men also consult with senior women despite the gendered norms that once adhered strictly in the context of *kujika*. They read the verses off paper, and from a computer screen, they open emails to access this information and practice in their homes, surrounded by very modern recording devices. But while this process is underway, they are heavily scrutinised by the community of remaining elders and middle-aged Yanyuwa who know another way of the Law; they encounter degrees of jealousy and admiration from their own and younger generations. They invoke memories of their mother's fathers and remember the old men who once sang, by listening to ethnographic recordings of their powerful voices. While they embark on this process, a commentary of voices chime in from the sidelines, prefaced by questions of whether they are doing the right thing, whether they are holding the Law adequately.

These young men are reworlding *kujika* and ceremony, with an audience that includes their human kin, their ancestral kin and their Country. As such they cannot invent or makeup Law, they must follow the path, as they are keenly aware of the multiple voices that must also surround the practice, recording and replay and eventual singing and performing, to put a song back into Country. To sing *kujika* is a huge undertaking of knowing family, knowing ancestral beings and knowing Country and the relational accord which binds each of these together through time.[4] As Gadrian Hoosan, a next generation Yanyuwa/Garrwa *kujika* man explains,

You know we bring this *kujika* back. We use paper, computer, we are recording, listening to the recording and practicing all the way. But in the end, it
is all family, it has to be brought back to family, it must be put back in the
ceremony place, we have to be following the Dreaming, that's the Law.
That's what we are trying to do, we don't have the old people anymore but
have to carry on, we can't let them down, so we try anyway what we reckon
is going to work. (2018)

Other examples of reworlding Law might be examined through land
rights, as part of a multi-pronged expression of cultural autonomy and
sovereignty, which seeks to redress threats to Indigenous Laws associated
with lands and waters, and resists harms against lands and waters as an
expression of responsibility and kinship. Land rights in this context are a
response to the historical event of land dispossession brought about by
colonisation, and the process through which one must fight for title is
determined and orchestrated by a white legal system. However, the imperative to act is based in the principles of Indigenous Law and kincentric
modalities, which prescribe relationships of responsiveness and action, all
of which is based in knowledge which requires praxis (Kearney 2018). All
forms of activism to safeguard Country might then be seen as a form of
reworlding, a demand born of the present moment to reinforce and practise Law over and above the intrusions which threaten to weaken or
destroy Country. Because Law itself is preeminent and is always in and of
the Yanyuwa world, it is the pathway by which to activate and enact care.

As witnessed by local efforts of young and mid-generation Yanyuwa,
organised local activism, focused on anti-mining, anti-fracking and the
imperative to safeguard Country and the health of local ecologies present
an alternative to legislative land rights. It demands ethical and just relations with Country and declares a self-determining space in which to
reworld Law through the asserting of culturally prescribed interests and
political commentary shaped by kinship and relationality. Activism is a
critical social site for interpreting the cultural complexity and power relations of public life, and for younger generations, it becomes a staging
ground for some of their first performances of knowledge based in Law.
Enshrined as a moral commitment, younger Yanyuwa continue to recognise the value of Law (Adgemis 2017, 2020; Kearney 2019), yet the
nature of what they know, how decisions are made about who might speak
and claim to know are more flexibly negotiated than they were in times

past. This signifies complexity in decision-making, choices and the compulsion to act in relation to Law.

Yanyuwa Law informs the political commentaries and voices of young activists, who are pushing to shift rhetoric around the need to safeguard ancestral lands and waters, for they contain the essence and actuality of the Dreaming (see Adgemis 2017, 2020). Yet, as the statements from Annie a-Karrakayny and Dinah Norman a-Marrngawi regarding permissions illustrate, there is now a generational distinction in negotiating the right to speak. Many younger people speak freely of Law when among peers and outsiders (including, e.g., non-Indigenous allies, politicians and audiences on social media), something which elders caution against. For elders there is diplomacy which must be practised if speaking of Law or purporting to know Law. This caution often leads to a refrain from speaking of Law among elders, in the full acknowledgement that certain people have the right to know, hold and share forms of knowledge and its Law. Young people thus might show a degree of caution in speaking forcefully of Law in the company of mid and elder generations, an audience which is known to scrutinise young people's understanding and proficiency with Law. This reveals a multi-generational consciousness of the rules that govern Law and the rights of certain people to speak in the company of others. It also highlights an awareness of consequence if the accepted praxis of Law is not followed.

There remains a high level of kin based political instruction, as well as displays of confidence and passivity across generations. Yet increasingly, for younger people in this community, the urgency of the threat to Law and specifically the health of Country demands action. This alteration in praxis requires a weighing up of the risks and potential harms that come with reworlding. Does new praxis cause detriment to the integrity of Law? Or is new praxis inherently led by the integrity of Law? The fact that we ask such questions highlights the continuation of a high stakes political choreography that comes with knowing, claiming to know and enacting Law.

Yanyuwa/Garrwa man Nicholas Fitzpatrick Milyari is keenly aware of the value of Law, Country and people, when he speaks to his motivation as a young activist,

> Our people are struggling a lot and have been for a while. We have a very high rate of suicide. We need help to revive and strengthen our cultures...This cannot be done if our land and water is wrecked forever by mining, gas, and oil companies. We are connected to the land – it is part of

us, and we are part of it. To destroy the land destroys us, and to destroy us destroys the land. The connection we have to this great country is very deep.... (Lock the Gate Alliance 2019)[5]

Gadrian Hoosan also contextualises the urge to participate in activism and explains the relationship between these choices and adherence to Law, attempting to firmly instate the overarching power and influence of Law at the centre of his activist motivation.

We live our laws, unchanging, because our laws and practices renew and sustain life…Government laws are about control and profit. We know there are Two Laws and respect that. But we live through our laws, that protect the water, that protect our kids, that unite us with the land and the source of life. The source of life comes from our creation stories – what the western world knows as the dreaming, our Yigan [Yijan], the source of life.

The Law that Yanyuwa seek to safeguard and reworld includes a continuity of cultural practices, including certain ceremonies, songlines, kinship, place names and land and sea tenure arrangements and management protocols as held by distinct clan groups. So too there is a high-level commitment to maintaining principles and practices of kincentric responsibility, obligation and sustained presence, depth of understanding and emotional care. Commitments to this vision of Law are today expressed through respect for older men and women, who are described as 'really knowing' because they lived and travelled over the land and sea and embodied Law throughout their lifetime. Senior members of the community are deemed essential to a process of Law recovery and care, yet it is through young people's praxis that Law will be held and maintained into the future. This is both a cause for hope and concern in the community.

Questions being asked by Yanyuwa include *what is Law today? How can the community straighten it up and teach it to young people? And how can the memories of old people be used to teach the young?* At present there are five remaining speakers of the Yanyuwa language and only one ceremony that is practised on an annual basis—the aforementioned *a-Marndiwa* male initiation ceremony. In the years leading up to the writing of this book, the Yanyuwa authors spoke often of these tensions between generational groups and how they understand and practise Law. They still highlight a prevailing need to revisit the meaning of Law in the present, relative to the lifestyles, pressures and opportunities which young people encounter. There is also a need to find ways of transmitting Law through direct person-to-person teaching activities and mentoring. Now that people have had access to a rich archive of documentary forms of Yanyuwa Law for over 20 years, they are more confident in interacting with Law in new ways and in stating what they do and don't know about. In order to teach the Law, elders express that there needs to be opportunity and context to share the knowledge that currently exists, to develop a deeper understanding of what Law might offer young people in the present, and to make high-stakes decisions about who will teach, what will be taught and how. The generational nature of knowledge sharing requires innovative approaches and heavy investment in knowledge building, through which people must learn before they can teach. In order for elder, mid and younger generations to participate in Law and Law education programs, there are several needs which must be met,

> That the knowledge of elders, including knowledge previously recorded by co-authors John and Amanda in collaboration with now deceased elders, is brought forward for the purposes of teaching.
>
> That elders make decisions about which aspects of Law might be appropriate for reinvigoration, weighing up present conditions which make it difficult or inappropriate to bring back secret and sacred practices.
>
> That mid generation Yanyuwa are given additional guidance in Law and how to teach it as emerging and future elders.
>
> That younger generations meet this Law for the first time in a culturally safe manner through mentoring with elders.

The reworlding of Law is heavily based in an ethical commitment to Country, based on performative intentionality. There is an ethical quality to Law that is demonstrated through dialogical not monological relationships, whereby humans adopt a stance of openness to notice and engage with their non-human kin, and hold room for emotional responsiveness to Country. Take, for example, an occasion on which Dinah Norman a-Marrngawi, who after an absence of three years, returned to her Country, to a place where her brother had tragically died. The day of arrival was spent calling out to Country and burning Country, but there was a strict instruction that no hunting should occur. The visit was about enacting the preliminaries of Law and associated protocols on returning to Country after a period of absence and specifically of returning to a place where someone has died.

On the following day Dinah went hunting at a nearby lagoon and brought back three small long-necked turtles (*murndangu*). As she sat cooking them alongside John Bradley, she abruptly stood up and called out to Country,

> *Wayi! Mili ngandarra barra? Marnajingarna a-nhanawaya ji-awarawu, karna-yirdardi marnaji ngarna barra a-wirriyarra ngarna a-nganji jiingku-mangaji ji-awarala. MIli ngandarra barra? Jina barra murndangu buyi barra buyi! Ngarna-nyngkarriya! Barni-ngalngandaya barra!*
> Hey! What is going on here? Here is I am a woman belonging to this Country, I grew up here, I am a person whose spirit comes from this Country, I am a kinswoman of this place. What is going on! These long-necked turtle are small, too small. Listen to me! Don't think you do not know me!

This is an expression of Law in action, an address to Country and unseen companions, the old people, the spirits of her deceased kin. Dinah invokes her relationship to place, her kinship to place and the expectations she in turn hopes to have validated by such a relationship. After she had called out she sat down and looking across the Country she saw a flock of galahs digging small tubers out of the ground. In response to this she called out,

> *Bajanda ngabiyarra a-ngulili aja-ngabuji, ngalangarna karna-wingkala ankaya yinda anmaya marnaji namba kurdardi ngarna yinda kantharra jina awara yinda rinkirinkimantharra kurdandu*
> There you are my kinswoman, the galah who is my most senior father's mother, when I return upriver (to Borroloola) you will remain here, when I am not here you will carry this Country, you will be lifting it up with intensity.

What is apparent is that there is a strong but small cohort of elders, and a small but growing number of younger men and women who are providing a spectrum of possible elaboration for a future of newly apprehended Law for Yanyuwa. In many remote communities there are younger men and women who are very capable of learning Law and when facing challenges often react and spontaneously position themselves and their Law within the shifting realm of their life. People are trying to bring Law back into focus, not as an abstract concept, nor a tightly defined legalistic concept but rather as an ongoing praxis. For Yanyuwa, Law is seen as a pathway to protection and nurturance for Country and people. Hence this book and its attention to Law is not an exercise in addressing loss but is about an engagement with cultural dynamism, which identifies the nature of Law as powerful, and enduring, but capable of change and reworlding.

STRENGTHS IN POLITICAL PLURALISM

Graham and Brigg (2020) have explored the strengths that might come with political pluralism in Australia, presenting a vision of Aboriginal political philosophy on generalist and for the most part accessible terms that might draw in a wider audience of listeners and students. Whilst some of the descriptions they provide for Aboriginal political concepts diverge from a Yanyuwa articulated vision of political and Law-based practice, there is a shared commitment to "more systematically describe and assert" distinct forms of socio-political ordering and governance. These distinct forms are multiple, for they are emplaced across Indigenous nations—that is across the linguistically and ancestrally distinct lands and waters which make up the landmass and waters of Australia.

Indigenous political concepts speak differently and speak back to the ideas which have come to govern this continent and others through waves of British and European colonial expansion (Graham and Briggs 2020). Graham and Briggs (2020) use a language of 'wisdom', 'ethics', 'autonomy', 'proportionality', 'Country', 'relationalism', 'autonomous regard' and 'relationist ethos'; but Yanyuwa use their own language, expressed as *narnu-yuwa* (lawfulness or correctness), kin and ancestral presence, *kujika* (songlines), the *a-yabala* (path, or road), *wurrama* (authority), *wirrimalaru* (power) and *ngalki* (essence), *linginmantharra* (being mindful) and *Yanyuwangala* (being Yanyuwa). There may or may not be English equivalents to each of these, and the translations noted in brackets may or may not suffice to reveal the depth and substance of Yanyuwa language and Law. But that is ok, because not everything should or could ever be mutually understandable or transposable across these distinct lifeworlds. There are also many other expressions and actions (ceremony, collective decision-making, consensus, orality) which distinguish Yanyuwa Law that we have not yet delved into in this book or have moved over quickly, based on the determinations of elders on what can be shared.

The point then, in presenting this account of Yanyuwa Law, is not to show everything but to demonstrate that multiple systems in Law co-exist and that there are benefits which come about through this co-existence. This view is what sustains a pluralist approach to political and legal regimes as forms of socio-political ordering and governance. As Chang (2012:261) explains, the dilemma of our time is one of "how do you choose what to believe?". But what if we are inclined, and also encouraged to instead ask, "how [and why] *do* you choose in any case". These questions alone are important steps in moving towards an ethical relation with Indigenous Laws and knowledges, and in seeking to understand something of the rigorous, complex and multiple forms of governance these provide for people and Country. There is a very long way to go before political pluralism is part of an accepted and formalised order of governance in Australia and other settler colonies. Thus, for now, simply accounting for the existence and realisation of political pluralism opens up pathways towards a conversation of new relational dispositions in a place like Australia.

In the case of Yanyuwa Law, collective decision-making practices, moral and ethical interactions with land and sea ownership, notions of testimony and rights and kincentricity as a relational expression of high political order are paramount. This is what governs people's everyday lives in this remote part of Australia, and is what shapes personhood, body politics, familial interactions, individual and communal freedoms, maturation and esteem building. For any decision-making that impacts on Yanyuwa lives, and for those who drive the decision-making processes (whether politicians, academics, policy-makers, doctors and healthcare workers, teachers or lawyers), the political life of this community provides the necessary and crucial insights for what will work and what will likely benefit Aboriginal people's lives.

As Yanyuwa continue to reworld their Law, it is certain that young people will be hoping, if not demanding, to see their own political structures and habits reflected in processes which govern their lives and futures. Younger generations of Yanyuwa are engaging with Law in new ways in the context of rapid change, yet the enduring potency and presence of Law in the Country holds that this revitalisation or reworlding is in substance a continuity of what has always governed their lives and Country. They do not engage with Law blindly but follow a path, and consider the implications of their praxis as it impacts upon Country, kin and ancestors. This is an exciting reality that will lead to the weighing up of different interpretations and courses of action for the practice of Law. And this book will serve as one instructional pathway in the process of continuous presence and steady reworlding.

NOTES

1. https://www.dfat.gov.au/about-us/publications/trade-investment/business-envoy/Pages/january-2019/indigenous-excellence-a-soft-power-asset-for-australia
2. The Northern Land Council is an independent statutory authority of the Commonwealth of Australia. It is responsible for assisting Aboriginal peoples in the Top End of the Northern Territory to acquire and manage their traditional lands and waters.
3. *a-Marndiwa* is a ceremony dedicated to transitioning young boys into manhood, whilst also solidifying kinship and putting families into important relationships of obligation and duty.
4. Singing *kujika* entails the learning of at least 300 separate verses, which must be sung in order. Singing a *kujika* in full may take at least 6 to 7 hours. They are sung at night and must end just before the sun rises.
5. To contextualise the Lock the Gate movement and community uptake of anti-fracking sentiments in Borroloola, see https://www.lockthegate.org.au/borroloola

REFERENCES

Adgemis, P. 2017. *We Are Yanyuwa – No Matter What: Town Life, Family and Change*. PhD Thesis, Monash University, Australia.

Adgemis, P. 2020. 'So did you find any culture up here mate?' Young men, 'deficit' and change. In A. Kearney and J. Bradley (Eds.) *Reflexive Ethnographic Practice: Three Generations of Social Researchers in One Place*. New York: Palgrave Macmillan, pp. 181–211.

Anderson, B., and Harrison, P. (Eds.). 2010. *Taking - Place: Non-representational Theories and Geography*. Farnham: Ashgate.

Australian Government, Department of Foreign Affairs and Trade. 2019. *Soft Power Assets for Australia*. Available at: https://www.dfat.gov.au/about-us/publications/trade-investment/business-envoy/Pages/january-2019/indigenous-excellence-a-soft-power-asset-for-australia, accessed May 17, 2022.

Carpenter, K., and Tsykarev, A. 2021. Indigenous peoples and diplomacy on the world stage. *AJIL Unbound* 115: 118–122. https://doi.org/10.1017/aju.2021.7

Chang, H. 2012. *Is Water H2O? Evidence, Realism and Pluralism*. New York: Springer.

Cropp, B. 1980. *This Rugged Coast*. Adelaide, South Australia: Rigby.

Graham, M., and Brigg, M. 2020. Why we need Aboriginal political philosophy now, more than ever. *ABC Religion & Ethics*. Australian Broadcasting Commission. Available at: https://www.abc.net.au/religion/why-we-need-aboriginal-political-philosophy/12865016

Grosfoguel, R. 2005. Hybridity and mestizaje: Sincretism or subversive complicity? Subalternity from the perspective of the coloniality of power. In A. Isfahani-Hammond (Ed.) *The Masters and the Slaves*. New York: Palgrave Macmillan, pp. 115–129.

Hoosan, G. 2018. *When Water Is Death – Indigenous X*. Available at: https://indigenousx.com.au/gadrian-hoosan-when-water-is-death/

Kearney, A. 2018. Returning to that which was never lost: Indigenous Australian saltwater identities, a history of Australian land claims and the paradox of return. *History and Anthropology* 29(2): 184–203. https://doi.org/10.1080/02757206.2017.1397646

Kearney, A. 2019. Interculturalism and responsive reflexivity in a settler colonial context. *Religions* 10: 199. Available at: https://www.mdpi.com/2077-1444/10/3/199. https://doi.org/10.3390/rel10030199

Kearney, A. 2021. *Keeping Company: An Anthropology of Being-In-Relation*. Abingdon, Oxon: Routledge.

Kulnieks, A., Roronhiakewen Longboat, D., and Young, K. 2013. *Contemporary Studies in Environmental and Indigenous Pedagogies: A Curricula of Stories and Place*. Rotterdam, The Netherlands: Sense Publishers.

Lock the Gate Alliance. 2019. *Gas Wars: Episode NT - Empire Must Not Frack*. September 5, 2019. Available at: https://www.lockthegate.org.au/gas_wars_episode_nt_empire_must_not_frack

Nader, L. (Ed.). 1996. *Naked Science: Anthropological Inquiry Into Boundaries, Power, and Knowledge*. London: Routledge.

Nelson, M., and Shilling, D. 2018. *Traditional Ecological Knowledge: Learning from Indigenous Practices for Environmental Sustainability*. Cambridge: Cambridge University Press.

Ridgeway, S., & Jacques, P. 2015. *Power of the Talking Stick: Indigenous politics and the world ecological crisis*. New York: Routledge.

Stewart, K. 2010. Worlding Refrains. In M. Gregg and G. Seigworth (Eds.) *The Affect Theory Reader*. London: Duke University Press, pp. 339–353.

Williams, L. 2021. *Indigenous Intergenerational Resilience: Confronting Cultural and Ecological Crisis*. Abingdon, Oxon: Routledge.

Yanyuwa Families, Bradley, J., and Cameron, N. 2003. *Forget About Flinders: An Indigenous Atlas of the Southwest Gulf of Carpentaria*. Canberra, NSW: Australian Institute of Aboriginal Studies.

CHAPTER 5

Conclusion

Abstract In the final chapter we conclude the book by restating the nature of Indigenous Law, as the localised configuration of a social, ecological, geographical and ancestral world. Law is held in language, song and ceremony, which delineate a people's physical and metaphysical territory. In contemporary colonised settings, Indigenous struggles for justice, sovereignty and self-determination are mediated through western frameworks and languages which erase the substance of Indigenous Law in and of itself. Indigenous people are faced with the dilemma of fighting for their family and their Country on terms and within systems that continue to obliterate and marginalise the realpolitik of their Law. In this concluding chapter we encourage researchers, artists, decision-makers, service providers and others who work with Indigenous peoples to seek out respectful relational encounters with Indigenous knowledges and Laws. This means forming relationships with people and communities in situ over extended periods of time wherever possible. As we have demonstrated, Indigenous Law continues to evolve and change in its manifestations between generations in the context of rapid socio-cultural change. However, Law also continues to govern the day-to-day negotiation of politics, people and identity within and between Indigenous communities. Decision-makers of all stripes working with Indigenous communities will benefit from a pluralistic disposition in seeking to better understand the communities they work alongside, and the Country on which they stand.

© The Author(s) 2023
A. Kearney et al., *Indigenous Law and the Politics of Kincentricity and Orality*, https://doi.org/10.1007/978-3-031-19239-5_5

Keywords Indigenous Law • Pluralism • Land rights • Law today

The southwest Gulf of Carpentaria occupies a particular place in the white Australian colonial imagination. The Gulf is a 'wild place' void of civilisation and culture; it was one of the 'final frontiers' of white settlement where pastoralists, explorers and various criminalised or socially objectionable outcasts 'tamed' a harsh and uninhabited part of the continent. Following the initial waves of white settlement, this region and in particular the township of Borroloola were widely perceived in the early-mid 1900s as a wild place of violence, criminality and unregulated pastoral development idiomatic of the 'real outback' (Harney 1946, 1957).

Yet, in a Yanyuwa registry, referring to a place or tracts of Country as 'wild' carries with it different connotations. In a Yanyuwa sense, 'wild Country' is Country that has been ruined, overrun, abandoned or overexploited, Country that has been thrashed by mining, tourism and agricultural development and is alienated from, and ultimately closed off to, the people who belong to it. The sea, rivers and vast savannahs yield less; land becomes overgrown and impenetrable; lagoons dry up, shrivel and become lifeless. People may remain in these places, yet they too dwindle and suffer as hearts grow wild with the grief for that which has been destroyed and the life that has been extinguished. In a Yanyuwa sense, wild Country is Country which no longer responds to, or is enlivened by, kinship and Law.

There is similarity between western and Yanyuwa perceptions of wildness, a general absence of life or lawfulness. From a western capitalist point of view, modern government, bureaucracy and regulation in the southwest Gulf of Carpentaria has facilitated agricultural and mining development throughout the twentieth century which has 'civilised' this once 'wild' place. Yet, in the Yanyuwa sense, during this time Country has become increasingly wild, wrecked, closed up and torn apart.

Indigenous Law is the localised configuration of a social, ecological, geographical and ancestral world. Law is held in language, song and ceremony, which delineate a people's physical and metaphysical territory. In contemporary colonised settings, Indigenous struggles for justice, sovereignty and self-determination are mediated through western frameworks and languages which erase the substance of Indigenous Law. Indigenous people are faced with the dilemma of fighting for their family and their Country on terms and within systems that continue to obliterate and marginalise the realpolitik of their Law. This tension manifests, for example, in the imposition of a 'stakeholder' framework in decision-making on Indigenous peoples' lands and waters. It is of little value for Indigenous people to be rendered as 'stakeholders' in their own Country, when those imposing this western democratic aesthetic in decision-making fail to comprehend what is ultimately *at stake* for Indigenous people.

Co-author and senior Yanyuwa Law man Graham Friday Dimanyurru spent many years as the head ranger of the li-Anthawirriyarra Sea Ranger Unit. Graham ceaselessly battled to convey to non-Indigenous bureaucrats, government representatives and legal functionaries what was at stake for his family and his community on Yanyuwa terms when being consulted about decisions impacting upon Yanyuwa Country. Throughout his life of advocacy and leadership in this community, Graham saw clearly how the placement of non-Indigenous law as the sole relevant mechanism for decision-making was at the heart of his community's perpetual hardship. In 2019, following a long meeting with representatives of the Parks and Wildlife Commission of the Northern Territory, the Northern Territory Government and the Australian Federal Government, Graham bluntly stated, "Whitefellas just have to pull Country apart, I have seen this. All of my life I have seen this, and I will tell you when whitefellas start this, there is no place for my Law, no, never!" To pull Country apart is to sever the bonds which we describe in this book; the kincentric web of relationships that holds Yanyuwa families and Country together, and further facilitates the continuity of Law between generations.

The legislative land rights schemes in Australia (including the *Native Title Act 1993* and the *Aboriginal Land Rights (Northern Territory) Act 1976*) are the most prominent attempt at integration of Indigenous 'custom', 'tradition' or Law into the Commonwealth's western or common law. Yet in this field, the depth of engagement with Indigenous Law is substantially limited within the parameters of western real property law. Land claims in this community have been sources of immense tension, grief, in-fighting and humiliation as Yanyuwa have been required to explain themselves and their Law on terms and in language which betrays the substance of their Law and knowledge. In 2000, Dinah Norman a-Marrngawi sat quietly with author John Bradley after a long day of giving evidence during the *Lhungkannguwarra – People of the Mangroves: Sea Country Claim* 2000. She reflected with fatigued intensity on the demand of having to explain the Law as she knew it to be within this whitefella western legal forum; a reflection upon what was really at stake.

> Do any of these whitefellas, really know how hard this Law is? What a big job it is? I have been holding it all day for these white people, holding the Law for this Country. Do they really understand how that is for me? I have to hold the Law and I have to hold all my family, and the Country, and the Dreamings, song, ceremony, old people, everything, I have to hold them. (Dinah Norman a-Marrngawi 2000)

The task of holding Country and Law together in this way is an immense job and existential battle, which challenges the continuity of Law between generations. Annie a-Karrakayny, a senior Yanyuwa Law woman in her time, and deeply philosophical thinker, likewise reflected on this situation some years earlier,

> ...whitefellas will never hold this Law (Yanyuwa Law), they have no idea, you listen now, how many whitefellas ever learn our language, so they might get ears... they just think we are plain stupid, dumb, but they are the ones got no idea, even big man like prime minister, lawyer, what do they really know... nothing... everything has to be made to suit them... always that way, whitefella always has to come out on top. (Annie a-Karrakayny 1982)

The case study of Yanyuwa Law and its flattened rendering within the legislative land rights systems demonstrates a fundamental tension. While a genuine understanding of Indigenous Law requires substantial time engaging with people in situ and the subsequent long-term development of relationships embedded within a localised community, too often the mechanisms which attempt to integrate Indigenous Law and knowledges into western law scarcely facilitate these prerequisites. This is to say nothing of the struggles in satisfying western demands for 'hard' evidence of a Law which is embedded in orality.

Old Arthur's testimony speaks to a level of intimate connectivity, reciprocity and responsibility among and between human and non-human phenomena; a deeply kincentric ecology built upon multilayered relationships that bind family to each other, to the Country and to place. Yanyuwa political agency and obligation does not stop at the edges of the human. Indigenous Law holds relationships between humans, their human and non-human ancestors, non-human presences such as animals and meteorological phenomena.

The Australia that many know today is demonstrated by a colonial map, and such maps divide land and sea into three categories: the border, the centre (the large cities, sites of power) and the outside (Thiong'o 1986:55). Through membership into one of these categories, we either receive the privileges associated with the centre, or become aware of the policies and erasures associated with violence on the periphery. We share Old Arthur's story as part of an exercise in remapping. Old Arthur's account of Law helps to restore Yanyuwa names, kinship and Law to the land and sea. Storytelling such as this begins and ends with a testimonial from, with and of Country. Country is not a backdrop to life, nor the context for a story, it is the very premise of why and how Law exists and why and how stories are told. Oral traditions are represented in this narrative, at the bequest of Annie a-Karrakayny, Old Arthur's sister's daughter. Their retelling is a process of reclamation that invokes oral and aural agents that speak to Yanyuwa sovereignty and decolonisation. Stories of Law such as presented in Chap. 3 are a creative force, grounded in relationality, revealing different political destinies, histories and geographies that are replete with narratives of Indigenous Law and politic, imagination and scholarship. There are elements of this reclamation and of Indigenous lifeworlds more broadly that the west will never grasp in depth.

This is not to say, however, that some degree of understanding and respectful engagement is not possible. At a deeper level, those who seek to understand Indigenous Law from an outsider perspective require a pluralistic and open disposition, a willingness to resist the urge to categorise knowledge and phenomena in accordance with a western way of being, and instead allow multiple ways of perceiving the world to co-exist. It is important to relinquish the urge to immediately make 'sense' of that which is foreign or incongruent with one's own way in the world. We encourage readers, researchers, decision-makers and non-Indigenous collaborators with Indigenous peoples to adopt a disposition of openness towards that which has no equivalence in one's own way of life, yet governs the lives of others alongside whom we live—or, indeed, on whose Country we live, work and grow.

Gradual insight into Indigenous Law on the part of non-Indigenous people is marked by moments where the disciplinary and epistemic boundaries which hold western knowledge in order tremor, shake and ultimately break apart. The flattening of Indigenous Law is analogous to the containment and redirection of water in Australia. Over centuries of white settlement on a substantially arid continent, Australia is now an agriculture of dams and vast irrigation schemes which foolhardily seek to manufacture a European landscape. Dams pockmark the Country, trapping water securely and redirecting it towards a Eurocentric design, artificially draining the Country. A genuine understanding of Indigenous Law is a releasing of the dam walls. Those who seek to understand Indigenous Law from a western viewpoint must allow the ordered world as they have constructed and known it to pour out from its becalmed containment—which reflects our own image on the surface—and allow it to cascade outward into suppressed and dried up tributaries, seeping into soil that that has been mapped but never truly been understood by the west.

A pluralist cultural and cognitive shift is the predicant for non-Indigenous audiences to understand Law as something beyond an ultimately inconsequential 'soft power' or esoteric origin story which holds no bearing on people and politics of the present. We encourage researchers, artists, decision-makers, service providers and others who work with Indigenous peoples to seek out respectful relational encounters with Indigenous knowledges and Laws. This means forming relationships with people and communities in situ over extended periods of time wherever possible. As we have demonstrated, Indigenous Law continues to evolve and change in its manifestations between generations in the context of rapid socio-cultural change. However, Law also continues to govern the day-to-day negotiation of politics, people and identity within and between Indigenous communities. Decision-makers of all stripes working with Indigenous communities will benefit from this disposition in seeking to better understand the communities they work alongside, and the Country on which they stand.

References

Harney, W. 1946. *North of 23°: Ramblings in North Australia*. Sydney, NSW: Australasian Publishing Company.

Harney, W. 1957. *Life Among the Aborigines*. London: Robert Hale Limited.

Thiong'o, N. 1986. *Decolonising the Mind: The Politics of Language in African Literature*. Nairobi: East African Education Publishers.

Index[1]

---

[1] Note: Page numbers followed by 'n' refer to notes.

A. Kearney et al., *Indigenous Law and the Politics of Kincentricity and Orality*, https://doi.org/10.1007/978-3-031-19239-5

Printed by Printforce, the Netherlands